Monroe County, West Virginia

DEATHS

1853–1870

Volume I

❧❧

Pauline Haga

Heritage Books
2024

HERITAGE BOOKS

AN IMPRINT OF HERITAGE BOOKS, INC.

Books, CDs, and more—Worldwide

For our listing of thousands of titles see our website
at
www.HeritageBooks.com

A Facsimile Reprint
Published 2024 by
HERITAGE BOOKS, INC.
Publishing Division
5810 Ruatan Street
Berwyn Heights, MD 20740

Originally published 2008

International Standard Book Number
Paperbound: 978-0-7884-7743-0

MONROE COUNTY DEATHS

VOLUME ONE

BY

PAULINE A. HAGA
BOX 1061
CRAB ORCHARD, W. VA. 25827

IN COMPILING THIS VOLUME ONE OF MONROE COUNTY DEATHS I
HAVE DISCOVERED THAT MONROE COUNTY KEPT SOME RECORDS
DURING THE YEARS OF THE CIVIL WAR.

DEATH RECORDS FOR THE YEAR OF 1862, WHICH ARE NOT IN
THE COURTHOUSE FILES WERE DISCOVERED ON SOME MICROFILM
IN THE ARCHIVES IN CHARLESTON. THEY APPEAR TO HAVE BEEN
COPIED FROM AN OLD LEDGER WHICH WAS TORN AND POSSIBLY
DAMAGED BY WATER. THE WRITING IS VERY HARD TO READ AND
TOOK SEVERAL HOURS TO TRANSCRIBE. SOME OF THE INFORMA-
TION HAD "FADED INTO HISTORY."

THESE DEATH RECORDS ARE ONLY THOSE REPORTED TO THE ASSE-
SSOR AS HE TRAVELED AROUND THE COUNTY EACH YEAR TO COM-
PILE THE NECESSARY RECORDS. A BOOK LATER ON MONROE CO-
UNTY CEMETERIES WILL GIVE MANY MORE DEATH RECORDS.

MONROE BECAME A COUNTY IN 1799 BUT DEATH RECORDS WERE NOT
KEPT UNTIL 1853 BY PASSAGE OF A LAW BY THE LEGISLATURE.

IT MAY BE POSSIBLE TO FIND OTHER DEATH RECORDS FOR THE
MISSING YEARS. IF SO THEY WILL BE REPORTED IN FUTURE VOL-
UMES.

WILLIAM M. NELSON

DIED IN

1859

BURIED AT UNION

1853

CATHARINE JOHNSON
DIED JULY 7th 1853 AGED 84 years

"Jesus said unto her I am the Resurrection and the life he that believeth on me though he were dead ye shall live.

Buried at Wolf Creek

MONROE COUNTY DEATHS

COMPILED BY

PAULINE A. HAGA

REGISTER

Lines Numbered.	NAME IN FULL.	WHITE.	COLORED.		NAME OF THE OWNER OF SLAVE.	SEX.		DATE OF DEATH.	PLACE OF DEATH.	NAME OF DISEASE, OR CAUSE OF DEATH.	AGE.		
			Free.	Slave.		Male.	Female.				Years.	Months.	Days.

YEAR OF 1853

1--Rachel Brown, 28, died July 12 at Brown's Mill of consumption, wife of William Brown. Born in Monroe County, daughter of Jacob and Catharine Honaker.

2--Nicholas Young died June 4 at Turkey Creek of cancer at age 62 years. Born in Pennsylvania, wife was Catharine Young. Reported by son, Lewis Young.

3--Mason, a slave belonging to Catherine Shanklin, died at age 16 years of a broken limb, which was amputated, near Union.

4--Thomas Cart Beamer died Jany 5 near Union at age 28 years of a liver complaint. Was son of John and Susan Beamer. Born at Second Creek, he was a blacksmith. His wife was Catharine Beamer.

5--John Riley Scott died Sept. 18 at Gap at age 1 year, 4 months of inflamation of lungs. Born in Giles Co. was son of George and Mary E. Scott.

6--Mary Jane Weaver, 11 years old, died Aug. 1 near Union of dropsy in head. Daughter of Aylett and Mary M. Weaver. Born in Botetourt Co., Va.

7--Mathew Cannaday died April 5 at the Poor House at age 47 years of affection of lungs. Born in Ireland, was a laborer. Reported by Daniel Vance, Keeper of the Poor House.

8--Franklin Stuart died Feb. 24 at the Poor House at age 26 years. Report said "burned by himself.." Born in Monroe Co. Reported by Daniel Vance, keeper of the Poor House.

9--Sarah Ann Young, 14, died at the Knobs, no cause listed. She was the daughter of Michael and Ellen R. Young.

10--Lucy Counts, 12, died Aug. 11 at the Bogs of measles. Was the daughter of Jno. A. and Angeline Counts.

11--Lucy Goodall, 54, died March 4 at Devil's Creek of consumption. Born in Orange Co., Va. was daughter of James and Mary Riddle. Her husband was James Gooddall.

12--Virinda Goodall, 17, died Feb. 17 at age 20 years, 10 months, 17 days of "congestion of the brain. She was the daughter of James and Lucy Goodall and born in Monroe County.

13--George Steel, age 72 years, 10 months, 29 days, died March 24 at Gap of dropsy in chest. Born in Pennsylvania was son of Thomas and Margaret Steel. Wife was Sarah Steel.

14--not named male, age one year, died at Dunlap's Creek of hives on Feb. 28 and was son of William L. and Elizabeth Mahon.

15--Betsy Ann Bostick, 15, died Jan. 11 on Waters of Second Creek of hives. Was daughter of Charles Allen and Martha Bostick.

16--Barbara Ann Fury, 2 years, 23 months, died Jany. 29 at Laurel Creek, daughter of Thos. and Ruth J. Fury.

17--John William Reed, 3 years old, died June 17 at Second Creek of measles. Son of Shanton and Lydia Reed.

18--Andrew L. R. Moss, no age listed, died June 20 at Second Creek of meales, son of Andrew and Virginia Moss.

19--Hendron Dickson, 23 years, died June 13 on Second Creek of a spinal affection. A painter, he was the son of Richard D. and Eliz. Dickson.

20--Peggy, a slave, belonging to Thomas Nickell died at Sinks at age 36 on Jany. 20 of "puerperal fever." Daughter of Harry and Fanny.

21--Sydney King, 36, died May 7 at Second Creek of measles. Consort was Jacob King. Born in Monroe daughter of James and Rebecca Martin.

22--Catharine Preston, 56 years, died Dec. 28 at Flat Mountain of apoplexy. Born in Augusta Co., Va., daughter of Hugh and Elenor Hanna. Reported by Martha Hanna, sister.

23--Mary Susan, 1 year, 4 months, slave of Mary Ann Nickell, died Sept. 20 at Sinks of flux. Daughter of Anthony and Bella.

24--Nancy Welch Terry, 65, died Nov. 17 at Knob of paralysis.
Born in Louisa Co., Va., daughter of Martin and Mary Dunn.
C. B. Terry, consort, reported death.

25--Thomas Alford, 82, died July 2 at Wolf Creek of old age.
Born in Rockingham Co., Va., a farmer. Death reported by
Mary Alford, daughter-in-law.

26--Robert Alford, 50, died at Wolf Creek Aug. 11. Born in
Monroe Co., was son of Thomas and Phebe Alford. A farmer,
his wife, Mary Alford, reported the death.

27--William Allen Thompson, 11 months, died of croup on Wolf
Creek, July 11, son of William and Caroline Thompson.

28--Isabella Miller, 75 years, 9 months, died Oct. 5 at Flat Mt.
of old age. Born in Scotland was daughter of Andrew and Margaret Miller. Reported by Consort, Andrew Miller.

29--William Lacy Boyd, 22, died Dec. 7 of consumption at Flat Mt.,
of consumption. Born at Sinks in Monroe he was son of Porterfield and Rachel Boyd. Wife, Mary Ann Boyd, reported death.

30--William, 20 year-old slave of Jno W. Lanius died June 30 at
Union. Born in Botetourt County, Va.

31--Isabella Francis, 16, died May 31 of disease of heart at
Union. Dau of James and Susan Francis.

32--Elizabeth Early, 26, died Oct. 16 of "dyepepsia" at Union.
Born in Monroe County was daughter of John and Ann Nickell.
Death reported by Daniel J. Early, consort.

33--Elizabeth Prentice, 74 years old, died Nov. 7 at paralysis.
Born in Pennsylvania was daughter of George and Jane Lynch.
Peggy Prentice, daughter, reported death.

34--Mary Jane Spangler, 3 years, 4 months, 9 days, died Aug. 2
at Union of croup, daughter of Lewis and Elizabeth Spangler.

35--Elizabeth Francis, 9, died of hives Feb. 10 at Union, daughter
of John E. and Eliz'th Francis. Born at Red Sulphur Springs.
Reported by Ann Harris, grandmother.

36--Charles, slave of Madison McDaniel, died Feb. 25 at age 3
years, 12 months of meales. Albert and Martha were parents.

37--not named female slave of Allen and Amanda, owned by Madison
McDaniel died March 20 at age 21 months of measles.

38--Ellen, 4 years old, slave of Frances Dunlap died Sept. 17 at
Union of dropsy in brain. Parents were Oliver and Mary.

39--Mary Virginia Campbell, 1 year, 10 months, died Aug. 18 at
    Sinks, daughter of Caperton and Barbara Campbell.

40--Martha Jane Campbell, 1 year, 10 months, died Aug. 18 at
    Sinks, daughter of Caperton and Barbara Campbell.

41--Julia, slave of William M. Patton, died at age 24 years, at
    Rocky Point of dropsy. Daughter of Hull and Betty and born
    in Monroe County.

42--Emma, slave of William M. Patton, died June 6 of diarrhea
    at age 5 months, daughter of Julia.

43--James William McDowell, 26 months, died of hives near Rocky
    Point, July 28, son of Richard and Mary A. McDowell.

44--William Early, 33, died Jany 30 near Rocky Point of hemorhage
    of lungs, son of Saml and Rebecca Early. Groom was shoemaker.
    Reproted by James Dunsmore, father-in-law.

45--William Wallace Early, one-year-old, died Sept. 11 near Rocky
    Point of measles, son of William and Hannah Early.

46--Nancy N. Hawkins, 18 years, 4 months, 20 days, died May 29 at
    Sinks of "perpual fever" reported by James Hawkins, consort.
    Daughter of John and Betty Nickell.

47--Elizabeth Jane Hawkins, 1 year, 5 months, died June 21 of
    "cholera Morbue" June 21 at Sinks, daughter of J. P. S. and
    Nancy Hawkins.

48--Lurenia Antionette Vance, 17 months, died Dec. 31 at Gap of
    hives, daughter of Adam and Cassan Vance.

49--Martha Jane Curry died at Union of consumption, daughter of
    John and Margaret George. Husband was George Washington
    Curry.

50--Not named female, 5 days old, died July 19 near Sweet Springs,
    prematurely born to Rich'd C. and Sarah A. Eggleston.

51--Mary B. Vines, 54 years, died of liver complain March 17 at
    Sinks. Born in Augusta Co., Va., daughter of Phillip Greg-
    ory. John Vines was husband. Reported by Eliza P. Vines,
    daughter-in-law.

52--Harriet, slave of Elizabeth Walker, died at age 1 year, 3
    months, near Union July 15. Mother was Martha Jane.

53--Philip, whose mother was Rachael, slave of Elizabeth Walker,
    died May 17 at 10 months near Union.

54--not named slave of Allen T. Caperton died in May of measles.
    Mother was Wirney.

55--Minda, 35 years, 1 day died Dec. 9 near Sweet Springs of
conumption, slave of Henry W. Moss.

56--Bella Magdaline Vance, 1 year, 2 days died Oct. 18 at Gap
of hives. Daughter of William and Mary Susan Vance.

57--William S. Foard, 2 years, 2 months, died April 17 at Springfield of pneumonia. Son of James A. and Jane Foard.

58--Eunice J. Ross, 13 days, died Sept. 22 at Laurel Creek of
juandice. Daughter of Robinson and B. E. Ross.

59--George T. Ballard, 7 years old, died of "croop" at Indian
Creek on Dec. 21. Son of Winslow and Sarah Ballard.

60--Elizabeth Kilburn, 62 years, 1 month, 19 days, died July 24
at Peters Mountain of dropsey, daughter of Isaac and Eliz'th
Kilburn. Born in Monroe County. Reported by Isaac Kilburn,
nephew.

61--Ann V. Cummins, 5 months, 24 days, died Aug. 26 at foot of
Peters Mountain of cholera morbis, daughter of Austin and Sarah
Cummins.

62--Lucinda Hutchison, 20 years, 2 months, 23 days, died Jan. 19
of conumption, daughter of Andrew and Nancy Hutchinson.

63--Milton Chambers, 1 month, 6 days, died of "croop" April 9 at
foot of Peters Mountain, son of James and Perlexany Chambers.

64--Loami Thompson, 1 year, 25 days, died July 25 at foot of Peters
Mountain of cholera Morbis, son of George and Melinda Thompson.

65--George Evans died in May of Croop at foot of Peters Mountain,
son of Thomas and Ellen Evans.

66--Andrew Fleshman, 9 years, 11 months, 19 days, died Dec. 14 at
foot of Peters Mountain of "St. Vitas Dance." Parents were
Elijah P. Fleshman.

67--Margaret Fry, 31 years, 11 months, 12 days, died May 16 at
Centerville of typhoid fever, wife of Isaac Fry. Born in Botetourt Co., Va., daughter of Philip and Jane Vass.

68--Nancy Upton, 72, died on Swopes Knob of "paralysis on May 11.
Born in Botetourt County, was wife of Loyd Upton. Daughter
of Joseph Anderson.

69--Banks, 25 years old, slave of A. and A. Dunlap and Co., died
Jan. 10 at Red Sulphur of inflamation of brain. Born in Monroe
Co., his occupation was a "ostler." Alex Haynes, oversser,
reported the death.

70--Mary E. Rutlege, 5 months, died at "Hands" Creek Oct. 27 of
bronchitis, daughter of Samuel and Adaline Rutledge.

71--Marion F. Ross, 2 years, 7 months, 25 days, died Sept. 18
   at Laurel Creek of "erysipilus." Daughter of John P. and
   Rebecca Ross.

72--No name, 3 month-old child died of pneumonia Oct. 7 at
   Indian Creek, parents being Andrew and Rhoda Mann.

73--Joseph, slave of Robert Thrasher, died Nov. 12 at Hands Creek
   of inflamtion of brain. Was 75 years old. Born in Campbell Co., Va. Wife was Hetty.

74--Hetty, 37 years, old, slave of Robert Thrasher died Nov. 18
   at Hands Creek. Husband was Joseph. Born Roanoke Co., Va.

75--James, 9 years old, slave of Robert Thrasher died Dec. 12 at
   Hands Creek, born in Monroe County.

76--Mary A. Campbell, 5 years, 11 months, died Feb. 25 of measles,
   child of Andrew Campbell.

77--Delany Swinney, 72 years old, died April 28 of dropsy. Born
   in Greenbrier County, wife was Percilla S. Death reported
   by james Swinney, son.

78--Peggy, slave of Harriet Stodghill, died at age 39 years, Dec.
   23 of inflamation of brain. C. Stodghill was master.

79--John Stone, 23 years old, died Jan. 2 at Centreville of typhoid fever, son of Eliza Johnson. Born in Botetourt Co.,
   Va. A hireling, he was employed by Anderson McNeer.

80--Mary J. Butt, 48, died Jan. 10 at
   Centreville of typhoid fever, wife
   of Shannon Butt. Born in Maryland
   was daughter of Steven Reece.

81--Emanuel M. Pence, 3 years, 2 mon-
   this, 3 days, died Jan. 20 at Indian Creek of croup, son of Moses
   and Delila Pence.

82--Haslet K. Riffe, 23 years, 7 months, died April 23 at Droping Creek of typhoid fever, son of Joel
   and Susan Riffe. Was a clerk.

Haslet K. Riffe

Buried at Droping Creek

83--Jane A. Kearns, 1 month, 1 day, died Dec. 25 at Peterstown of scarlet fever, daughter of Jacob and Eliz'th Kearns.

84--Andrew J. Bowman, 16 years, 11 months, died May 11 at Brush Creek from a fall, son of Samuel Bowman. Born in Rockingham Co., Va.

85--Milam Pennington, 21 years, 11 months, died on New River May 18 of fever, son of William Pennington.

86--Harrison Pennington, 15 years, 5 months, died of flux Sept. 1 on New River, son of William Pennington.

87--Nancy Powley, 34 years old, died Aug. 31 on New River of flux. Born in Giles County, daughter of Jonathan Powley. Reported by William Pennington, neighbor.

88--William A. Powley, 5 months, died Sept. 23 on New River of flux, son of Nancy Powley. Reported by a neighbor, William Pennington.

89--Thomas Walker, 90 years, died of old age on New River Nov. 7. Born in Monroe County was son of Thomas Walker. Wife was Eleanor W. Walker. Reported by Alex'd Walker, nephew.

90--A one-month-old slave owned by Mary Walker died Dec. 29 on New River. Alexander Walker was master.

91--Brooker Thompson, 29 years, 9 months, 1 day, died Sept. 2 on Brush Creek of consumption. Born in Monroe County, was son of Logan and Nancy Thompson. Wife was Emily Thompson.

92--Alexander Dunlap, 40 years, 11 months, 11 days, died March 1 at Red Sulphur of liver disease. Born in Monroe County, son of Alexander Dunlap Sr. Was a merchant. Wife was Mary Ann Dunlap. Reported by Alexander Haynes, nephew.

93--Virginia A. Dunlap, 11 year, 10 months, 27 days, died April 22, son of Alexander and Mary A. Dunlap. Reproted by Alexander Haynes, nephew.

94--Jenny, slave owned by Mary A. Dunlap died May 7 at Red Sulphur of fever, reported by Alexander Haynes.

95--Mahala J. Canterbury, 4 months, 15 days, died Sept. 30 at Hans Creek of pneumonia, daughter of John and Eliz'th Canterbury.

96--John C. Green died Dec. 3 at Hans Creek of penumonia at age 4 months, 3 days, son of Whitson and Elizabeth Green.

97-- Elizabeth Campbell, 68, died June 10 at Indian Creek of cholera. Born In Pennsylvania, was daughter of Thomas Steele. Samuel Campbell, husband, gave information.

98--Henry S. Adair, 9 months, died Jan. 7 at Red Sulphur of "teething." Was son of William and Sarah Adair.

99--Rhoda, 45, slave of William Adair, died Aug. 9 of disease of head. Born in Richmond, Va.

100--John, slave of William Adair died July 25 at age 1 year, 15 days at Red Sulphur of scrofula. Born in Monroe County to Rhoda.

101--10-month-old female child of Jackson Garten died at Wolf Creek Dec. 3.

102--Female child of Thomas and Nancy Crawford died April 20 at Wolf Creek.

103--Fielding J. Crawford, 1 year, 11 months, 14 days, died May 29 at croup, son of Thos. and Nancy Crawford.

104--John Mann Jr. died at Indian Creek Nov. 2 of rheumatism, age 44 years, 6 months. Born in Monroe County, son of Adam and Mary Mann. Wife was Elizabeth Mann.

105--Newton A. Hill, 19 years, 6 months, died Oct. 25 on Greenbrier River of consumption. Born in Monroe County, son of James T. and Mary Hill.

106--Catharine Johnson, 86, died of old age July 7 at Crop Roads, reported by Caleb Johnson, son. Born in Augusta Co., Va., daughter of Jacob and Catharine Doran. Robert Johnson was husband.

107--John Alford, 80, died of dropsy April 15 at Wolf Creek. Born in Rockingham Co., Va., son of John and Jane Alford. Wife was Margaret Alford. Reported by son, Thomas Alford.

108--Female, one month, 7 days, died at Wolf Creek July 13, child of Wesley and Fanny Atha.

109--Charles Maddy, 43 years, 4 months, 16 days, died Jan. 16 at Laurel Creek of typhoid fever. Born in Monroe Co., son of John and Barbara Maddy. Wife was Margaret Maddy. Reported by John Maddy, brother.

110--Richard McNeer, 68 years, 1 month, 3 days, died Aug. 19 at Hans Creek of cancer. Born in Monroe County, was son of James and Eliz'th McNeer. Wife was Elizabeth McNeer. Death reported by son, Anderson McNeer.

111--John Henry, 4 months, slave of Richard McNeer died May 4 of fits. Parents were Robt. and Mahula Fulton.

112--Mary E. Foster, 8 years, died Sept. 15 on Greenbrier River, daughter of James and Nancy Foster.

113--Stephen Noble, 22 years, 15 days, died July 19 on New River of typhoid fever, son of Weley and Nancy Noble. Wife was Lucy E. Noble. Occupation was hireling.

114--Elizabeth Meadows, 21 years, 6 months, died May 19 on the Greenbrier River of pneumonia. Born in Monroe County, was daughter of James and Eliza Robinson. Husband was Paris Meadows.

115--William Pembroke, slave of Joseph F. Maddy, 3 years old, died Sept. 30 of measles. Mother was Jane.

116--Nancy R. Maddy, 3 years, 11 months, 20 days, died May 8 of measles, daughter of Absolem and Elizabeth Maddy.

117--Sarah S. Mann, 20 years, 6 months, 25 days, died Aug. 9 at Springfield of fits. Husband was Chris Mann. Born Monroe County, was daughter of Benjamin and Rebecca Peck.

118--Anthony, 30, slave of Delany Swinney, died Jan. 18 at Springfield. Was poisoned. Born in Pittsylvania Co., Va. Henry Mann, master, reported the death.

119--Lucinda Wykle, 37 years, 7 months, died June 9 at Farms of consumption. Husband was Geroge Wykle. Born in Monroe County, was daughter of Henry and Ann Smith.

120--Edwin W. Woodson, 45 years, 4 months, died May 14 at Farms of pneumonia. Born in Cumberland County, was son of John and Mary Woodson. Adaline B. Woodson was wife.

121--Sarah Meriday, 17 years, died Aug. 7 at Wolf Creek of typhoid fever. Husband was Joseph Meredy (spelled two ways) Born in Monroe County was daughter of George Wallers.

122--Moses Mann, 48, died Dec. 12 at Brush Creek of fever. Born in Monroe County, was son of Jacob and Mary Mann. Wife was Eliza Mann.

123--Sarah A. Waller, 20, died at Wolf Creek of cold on May 25, wife of Davna Waller. Born in Monroe County, daughter of John and Mary Ripley.

124--Barbara Hines, 60 years, 1 months, 25 days, died Oct. 4 at Wolf Creek of fever. Born in Monroe County, was daughter of Joseph Haynes. William Hines was husband.

125--female, 21 days old, died May 6 at Wolf Creek, child of James Dempsey.

126--Samuel M. Bobbitt, 21 days, died Aug. 10 at Wolf Creek, son of Oregan and Lucy Bobbitt. Born in Greenbrier County. Reported by grandfahter, Francis Hill.

127--William P. Stickler, 11 months, 25 days, died Dec. 10 on Greenbrier River of "phthisie." Born in Kanawha County, son of Lewis and Caroline Stickler.

128--Lewis Johnson, 24 years, 2 months, died July 20 on Greenbrier River of inflamation of bowels. A merchant, he was son of Jacob and Virginia Johnson. Virginia Johnson was wife.

129--Elizabeth Ellison, 46 years, died April 24 at Farms of fever. Francis Ellison was husband. Daughter of John Peters Jr., she was born in Monroe County.

130--male, 6 days old, died July 23 at Sprinfield, child of Geo. B. and Elizabeth Mann.

131--Eliza G. Gibson, 1 year, 6 months, 2 days, died Aug. 17 at Springfield, daughter of Adam and M. J. Gibson.

132--Rebecca J. Miller, 5 months, died April 28 at Springfield of measles, daughter of Rufus and Mary M. Miller.

133--Conrad Deboy, 77 years, died July 10 at Wolf Creek of "dis-popsin." Born in Monroe County, son of John and Elizabeth Deboy. Jane Deboy was wife.

134--Siba F. Craft, 8 months, 12 days, died Oct. 27 on Greenbrier River of croup, daughter of Jas M. and Eliz't Craft. Born in Botetourt Co., Va. Reported by William M. Selvey, neighbor.

135--Sarah Selvey 26, died Aug. 9 on Greenbrier River of "bilious" fever. Born in Botetourt Co., Va., daughter of Jas. M. and Elizabeth Craft. Reported by William M. Selvey, husband.

136--James M. Selvey, 3 years, 8 months, died Nov. 15 of scarlet fever, son of William M. and Sarah Selvey. Born in Monroe Co.

137--Joshua Curt, 3 years old, died June 10 on Greenbrier River of measles, son of William C. and Eliz'th Curt. Reported by William M. Selvey, relation.

138--Laonides H. Allen died May 7, son of Nathaniel and Sarah Allen.

139--Two day old male child of Joseph and E. Bragg died Dec. 15 on Keeneys Knob of diarrhea.

140--William Taylor, 46 years, 4 months, died Feb. 17 at Wolf Creek of diarrhea. Born in Monroe County, son of William and Catharine Taylor. (Was idiot)

MONROE COUNTY DEATHS
YEAR OF 1853

141--Francis Meadows, 80 years old, died Feb. 8 on Greenbrier
    River of old age. Born in Monroe County, was daughter of
    John and Kiseah Bush. Husband was Francis Meadows. Death
    reported by a son, Nathan Meadows.

142--Caroline R. Mann, 2 years, 11 months, died Dec. 30 at
    Centerville, daughter of Isaac and Nancy Mann.

143--female died June 6 on New River, child of Wesley and Fanny
    Atha.

144--male died March 8 at Rich Creek, child of William C. Riner.

145--Harry, slave of Jas M. Haynes died Jan. 10 at age 64 years,
    8 months on the Greenbrier River, son of Jane.

146--Henry, slave of Jas M. Haynes, 3 months old, died July 16
    of croup on the Greenbrier River.

147--Joseph Ellison, 64 years, 8 months, 17 days, died Oct, 11
    at Hans Creek of rheumatism. Born in Monroe County, son of
    John and Fanny Ellison. Wife was Jane Ellison. Death rep-
    orted by son, Wesley Ellison.

148--Jane Ellison, 62 years, 11 month, 8 days, died Nov. 23 at
    Hans Creek of "apoplexy." Was wife of Joseph Ellison. Death
    reported by a son, Wesley Ellison. Born in Monroe County
    was daughter of Saml. and Martha Garven.

Francis Meadows? At Peterstown Cemetery in
Meadows plot

1854

A. C. SHANKLIN
DEC. (DECEASED) MARCH THE 31
1854--AGE 24 YEARS, 4 MONTHS
28 DAYS

1--William W. Barger, 2 months, 8 days, died Oct. 30 of bold
hives, was child of William and Mary J. Barger.

2--Ann Broyles, 54, died March 31 of "diareah." Unmarried,
she was the daughter of Zachary and Eliz. Broyles. Death
was reported by her step-mother, Susan Broyles.

3--Elizabeth Bailey, 22, died Oct. 2 of consumption. Wife of
James M. Bailey. Born in Monroe County, daughter of Samuel J. and Cinthea Hutchison.

4--William M. Ballard, 6 months old, died Dec. 9 of scarlet
fever, son of John and Julia A. Ballard.

5--Newton J. Bair, 2 years, 10 months, 11 days, died Dec. 3
of disease of liver. Son of Jacob and Eliz. P. Bair.

6--Frances Bragg, daughter of Joseph and Eliz'h Bragg, died
Aug. 17 of "diareah."

7--Susan Buckland died sudden at age 49 years Feb. 14. Unmarr-
ied, death was reported by a sister, Elizabeth Buckland.
Born in Rockingham City, she was daughter of John and
Susan Buckland.

8--William H. Chatman, 4 months died Dec. 5, illness not known,
son of Samuel and Mary A. Chathan , (spelled two ways).
Reported by Isaac H. Mann, uncle.

9--John S. Campbell, 2 years, 8 months, 19 days, died Dec. 26
of scarlet fever, son of Robert and Mary C. Campbell.

10--Parthena Clower, 3 years, 8 months, 16 days, died Dec. 26
of scarlet fever. Born in Pulaski County, Va., daughter
of Daniel and Parthena Clower.

11--Floyd Crawford, 32, died April 11 of fever, husband of
Martha Crawford. Born in Monroe County, son of Thos and
Polly Crawford.

12--Mary F. Crews, 6 years, died Dec. 7 of "dipentery." Born
In Monore County, daughter of Sedley and Eveline Crews.

13--Mary A. Chatman, 2 months, 9 days, died Nov. 16 of not
known cause, daughter of Samuel and Mary A. Chatman.

14--Alex' C. Mann, 5 months, 22 days, died July 9 of croup,
son of Eli and Nancy Mann.

15--Dicey Cummins, 76, died sudden June 5. Born in Albermarle
Co., Va., daughter of Chas. and Ann Brooken. Reported by
Henry Miller, grandson.

16--female died June 25, child of William S. and Winney
   Dempsey.

17--Thomas Dunbar, 59 years, 5 months, 7 days, died Aug. 13
   of "bilious cholic.: Born in Botetourt Co., son of Robert and Hannah Dunbar. Mary Dunbar was wife.

18--George Dillion, 2 years, 7 months, 4 days, died Oct. 9
   of scarlet fever, son of Quince and Catharine Dillion.

19--David Diddle, 70 years, 4 months, 6 days, died Dec. 15
   of consumption. Born in Augusta Co., Va., was son of John
   L. Diddle. Wife was Catharine Diddle.

20--Jane Deboie, 75, died consumption August her death reported
   by Susan Deboie, daughter. Husband was Conred Deboie.

21--Sarah Dick, 70, died of palsy March 24, death reported by
   a daughter, Mildred Lively. Husband was William Dick.

22--Delila Eads, 30, died Nov. 27 giving birth, death reported
   by husband, John Eads. Born in Botetourt Co., Va., daughter of Samuel and Delila Eady.

23--Polly Erskine, 49 years, 5 months, 10 days, died Aug. 28
   of cancer, wife of Charles Erskine. Born in Monroe County,
   daughter of Thomas and Mary McCarty. Reported by daughter,
   Catharine Erskine.

24--Jane E. Faudree, 4 years, 10 months, died Dec. 20 of scarlet fever. Daughter of Richard and Francis Faudree.

25--Mary E. Gibson, 6 months, died July 15, daughter of Adam
   and M. J. Gibson. Reported by Isaac H. Mann, cousin.

26--Lucy C. Gray died Aug. 19 of cold, daughter of James W.
   and Eliz. Gray

27--J. S. Gwinn, 24 years, 10 months, 14 days, died Dec. 9 of
   pneumonia. Born in Monroe County, was a merchant, son of
   Andrew and Mary Gwinn. Was unmarried.

28--Mary J. Gibson, 20, died Feb. 24 of fever, wife of Adam
   Gibson. Born in Monroe Co., daughter of Moses and Sarah
   Mann. Death reported by Adam Mann, cousin.

29--Mary E. Gibson, 6 years, 5 months, died of inflamation of
   brain July 15, daughter of Adam and M. J. Gibson. Reported
   by Adam Mann, cousin.

30--Jane Graham, 43 years, 3 months, 22 days, died July 28.
   Death report said "murdered." Born in Monroe County, was
   daughter of Jos. and Rebecca Graham. Unmarried.

31--Preston Hargo, 7 years, died in November of inflamation of brain, son of Edward Goodwin and Cath. Hargo.

32--Sarah E. Hecht, died of whooping cough Feb. 20. Born Monroe County, daughter of John and Mary Hecht. Was 11 months old.

33--Sarah Humphreys, 76, died March 30 of "cholic. Husband was Saml. Humphreys. Born in North Carolina was daughter of Daniel and Nancy Jaroins.

34--George W. Hutchison, 9 years, 21 days, was "kicked by colt," and died Aug. 20. Son of Jno. M. and Malinda Hutchison.

35--Laura A. Hull, 1 year, 2 months, died of unknown illness on Dec. 19. Daughter of Anderson and Nancy J. Hull.

36--William Herron, 1 year, 4 months, died of whooping cough on Mch. 11, son of William and Mary Herron.

37--Mary M. Humphreys, 6 years, 8 months, 6 days, died Dec. 17 of scarlet fever, daughter of S. C. and Isabel M. Humphreys.

38--Samuel C. Humphreys, 4 years, 7 months, 8 days, died scarlet fever Dec. 24 son of Samuel C. Humphreys.

39--Lucinda Hutchison, 20 years, 3 days, died consumption Jan. 19 daughter of Andrew and Nancy Hutchison.

40--Geo. W. Harvey, 6 months, 15 days, died September 24 of flux, son of Jonathan H. and Lucinda Harvey.

41--Jas. R. Harvey, 6 years, 7 months, 15 days, died Aug. 31 of flux, son of James S. and Eliza Harvey.

42--Rhoda, 45, slave of Jos. K. Hill died Aug. 10 of not known illness.

43--Edward D. Hill, 7 years, 2 months, 6 days, died Feb. 14 of croup, son of James T. and Mary Hill.

44--Richard Johnson, 6 years, 6 months, 25 days, died Sept. 15 of flux, son of Thos. R. and C. W. Johnson.

45--Harriet W. Johnson, 10 years, 9 months, 27 days, died Sept. 17 of flux, son of Thos. R. and C. W. Johnson.

46--Clarenda E. Jones, 14, died Nov. 23 of scarlet fever, daughter of Chs. E. and Eliz'th Jones.

47--Lucy Knode, 32, died April 10 of dropsy. Born in Monroe Co., daughter of James and Jane Ballard. Death reported by William Smith, friend.

48--Chs. W. Lively, 5 months, 28 days, died Nov. 14 of scarlet fever, son of Wilson and Eliza Lively.

YEAR OF 1854

49--John A. Lowe, 6 years, 20 days, died April 16 of scarlet
    fever, son of Alex'n and Adaline Lowe.
50--Chs. L. Lowe, 8 months, 21 days, died April 20 of scarlet
    fever, son of Alex'n and Adaline Lowe.

51--Rupard N. Lively, 3 years, 8 months, 25 days, died April
    25 of flux, son of Jordan and Cyntha Lively.
52--Sidney M. Lively, 11 years, 6 months, 24 days, died Oct.
    9 of flux, son of Jordan and Cyntha Lively.

53--Eliz E. Maddy, 6 years, died Oct. 19 of dysentary, daugh-
    ter of Chs. and Margaret Maddy. Reported by Shannon Butt,
    step-father.

54--Michael G. Miller, 18 years, 10 months, 15 days, died March
    26 of 'disease of the heart." Son of Thos. and Sarah Miller.

55--Martha A. Maiys, 34, died of consumption Aug. 28. Born in
    Amherst County husband was Edward P. Mays. (spelled both
    ways). Daughter of Job and Adalien Carter.

56--Nancy C. Meadows, 3 years, 7 months, 7 days died of scarlet
    fever Dec. 23, daughter of Ro. and Isabel Meadows.

57--Amanda Meadows , 19, died of disease of bowels Sept. 20, wife
    of Allen Meadows. Daughter of Jas and Magdalen Boon.

58--Polly Martin, 43, died sudden Sept. 20, daughter of Jno. and
    Mildred Martin. Born in Franklin County. Unmarried, death
    reported by a sister, Judy Garten.

59--Allen G. Mann, 2 years, 4 months, 10 days, died of croup
    Feb. 4, son of Jno. M. and Jane Mann.

60--Rhoda Miller, 76, died of old age July 28. Born in Albermarle
    County, daughter of Chs. and Ann Brooklin. Death reported by
    Henry Miller, grandson.

61--Mary E. Mann, 12 days, died of unknown illness Feb. 19, dau-
    ghter of Jno M. and Jane Mann.

62--Nancy W. Mann, 55 years, 4 months, died of dysentary Oct. 14.
    James Mann Jr. was husband. Born in Monroe County, daughter
    of Saml. and Mary Humphreys.

63--Albert Mann, 20, died of consumption Aug. 27, son of James and
    Nancy W. Mann.

64--Ward C. Mann, 18, died of fever May 10, son of Alexander
    and Isabel Mann. Was tailer.

65--Christopher Mann, 23 years, 2 months, 17 days, died of
    fever March 12, son of Henry and Malinda Mann.

66--Rhoda Mann, 16 years old, died Feb. 8 of fever, daughter
    of William and Sarah Mann.

67--Elizabeth Mead, 50 years, 5 months, 4 days, died April 17
    of typhoid fever. Born in Pittsylvania County, was wife
    of M. Mead. Death reported by daughter, Mary A. Campbell.
    Daughter of Newton and Rachel Ramsey.

68--William H. Mann died April 30 in Kentucky at age 19 years,
    4 months and 21 days. Was a wood chopper. Born in Monroe
    County, son of Jefferson and Rebecca Mann.

69--Amanda Page, 11 months, died May 12, was burned, daughter
    of Thos. J. and Sarah Page.

70--Elizabeth Payne, 23 years, 7 months, 24 days, died May 7
    of dropsy, daughter of Henry and Charlotte Payne.

71--Henderson Rains died in Sept. of flux at age 12 years.
    Son of John and Nancy Rains.
72--Eliza Rains, 1 year, 10 months, died Sept. of flux, daughter
    of John and Nancy Rains.

73--Leah Rains, 33 years, 12 days, died Sept. 12 of flux, wife
    of Caleb Rains. Born in Monroe County, daughter of Joshua
    and Sarah Harvey.

74--Catharine Ryan, 5 years old, died July 14 of flux, daughter
    of John and Mary Ryan.
75--George Ryan, 15 days died (no date given), son of John and
    Mary Ryan.

76--William Smith, 74, died of old age March 26. Born in Bath
    County, Va., was son of William and Ellen Smith. His wife
    was Ellen Smith. Reported by a son, William Smith.

77--Thomas Smithson, 81 years old, died Oct. 9 of old age.
    Born in Maryland, son of Thos. and Sarah Smithson. Was a
    stone mason. Wife was Margaret Smithson. Reported by A. G.
    Alderson, nephew.

78--Alex'n C. Shanklin, 24, died of fever on March 26.
    Was a son of Absolem and Nancy Shanklin. Occupation was
    constable. Wife was Olivia Shanklin.

79--Virginia A. Shanklin, 5 months, died in September of dysen-
    tary, daughter of A. C. and Olivia Shanklin.

80--Phebe C. Swope, 2 years, 4 months, died of dysentary on
    Sept. 11, daughter of David R. and N. M. Swope.

81--Eliz'h M. Smith, 4 years, 11 months, died of fever May 3,
    daughter of Landon and Eveline Smith.

82--Arabel E. Smith, 3 years, 4 months, died of fever May 10,
    daughter of Landon and Eveline Smith.
83--Martha S. Smith, 1 year, 6 months, died of "hooping cough"
    June 27, daughter of Landon and Eveline Smith.

84--Emily Toler, 7 years, 2 months and 18 days, died of flux
    Aug. 30, daughter of C. B. and Nancy Toler.
85--Sarah J Toler, 11 years, 4 months, 23 days, died Sept. 7
    of flux, dau of C. B. and Nancy Toler.
86--Erastus Toler, 10 months, died Oct. 15 of flux, son of C.
    B. and Nancy Toler.

87--William P. Tuggle, 4 years, 3 months, 7 days, died Nov. 20
    of scarlet fever, son of Larkin and Isabel Tuggle. Born in
    Mercer County.
88--Margaret M. Tuggle, 2 years, 11 months, 23 days, died Nov.
    20 of scarlet fever, daughter of Larkin and Isabel Tuggle.
    Born in Mercer County.

89--Elizabeth Thompson, 1 year, 7 months, died Sept. 29 of
    "dysentary." Daughter of Geo. A. and Amanda Thompson.

90--John H. Trent, 11 years, died of "hooping cough," in Feb-
    ruary. Son of Jessee and Lucinda Trent. Born in Franklin
    County, Va.

91--Rebecca Jane Vass, 2 years, 11 months, 3 days, died April
    8 of inflamation of the brain, daughter of Isaac and Nancy
    Vass.
92--Ebro Willy Vass, 6 years, 11 months, 4 days, died Dec. 14
    of scarlet fever, son of Isaac and Nancy Vass.

93--Margaret Wikle, 28 years, 3 months, 23 days, died Dec. 24.
    Husband was Geo C. Wykel. Born in Monroe County, daughter
    of William and Eliz'h Donaldson.

94--Martha A. Wiseman, 2 years, 9 months, 1 day, died Dec. 28
    of scarlet fever. Parents were Henry J. and Nancy Wise-
    man.

95--Lewis Williams, 2 years, 4 months, 21 days, died Jan. 16
    of scarlet fever, son of Folesi and Nancy Williams.

96--Mary M. Wiseman, 30, died March 16 of consumption, wife of
    Thos. Wiseman. Born in Monroe County, daughter of Geo. and
    Mary Stevenson.

97--Thos. J. Wiseman, 4 days old, died May 5, child of Thos.
    and Mary M. Wiseman.

98--Neivel J. Woodram, 8 years, 8 days, died June 8 of penu-
    monia, daughter of John and Juda Woodram.

99--John H. Ewing, 9 years old, died July 20. Born in Nicholas
    County, son of Elisha and M. A. Ewing.

100--2-month-old slave of John Skaggs died in April.

101--Elie Miller, 7 years old, died Sept. 13 of liver complaint, daughter of Peter and Mary Miller.

102--Eunice A. Coffman, 14 months, died Aug. 6 of inflamation of the bowels, daughter of A. J. and S. E. Coffman.

103--Mary A. Dunsmore, 20 years, 3 months, 11 days, died Sept.
16 of consumption. Daughter of W. E. and Holmes. Death
reported by husband, William H. Dunsmore.

104--William Erskine, 24 years, 3 months, died Sept. 3 of
consumption, son of Jas. and Ellen Erskine. Death reported
by a friend, Robert Boyd.

105--David C. Nickell, 3 years, 2 months, 13 days, died Oct. 28
of croup, son of John A. and M. J. Nickell.

106--Caroline S. Ballard, 11 months, died Sept. 16 of whooping
cough, daughter of R. and Agnes Ballard.

107--Julia Long, 36, died Feb. 11 of consumption, wife of William Long. Born in Bedford County, Va., daughter of John
and Mary Dowdy.

108--Hugh L. Lynch, 7 years, 3 months, 11 days, died Sept. 1
of ulcer, son of Jno C. and Ann Lynch.

109--4 month, 9 day old son of A. H. and M. M. Neel died Dec.
18. Also had S. H. Neel as name of father.

110--Hannah Leach, 78 years, 5 months, 3 days, died Dec. 13
of dropsy. death reported by a son, Edmund Leach. Daughter
of William and Frances Hawkins.

111--George Lowe, 43, died of typhoid fever, death reported by
a sister, Eliz'th Lowe. Son of Z. and M. Lowe.

112--James Young, 62 years, 8 months, died Oct. 10 of disease
of the heart, son of R. and L. Young. Reported by a brother, William Young.

113--Susan Beamer, 58 years, 4 months, 10 days, died July 3
of dropsy. Born in Greenbrier County, was daughter of Adam
and C. Cart. Husband was John Beamer.

114--Elizabeth McGlamery, 68 years, died March 23 of disease
of the heart. Born in Augusta County, Va. was daughter of
Jno. and Isabel McGlamery. Reported by H. Hogshead, a
nephew.

115--Andrew Ballentine, 90, died of old age Dec. 20. Born in
Scotland.

116--John Humphreys, 42, died Nov. 30 of disease of the heart.
Lucy Humphreys was wife. Born in Monroe County was son of
H. M. Humphreys.

117--Alice J., 2 years, 11 months, slave of Lewis Campbell, died
Dec. 15. Mother was Agness.

118--Georgiana Wayte, 23, died of consumption. Death reported by
F. Hall, a friend.

119--James Foster, 21 years, 9 months, 8 days died Aug. 10 of
flux, born in Nicholas County, son of Isaac Foster. Wife
was Mahala Foster.

120--Mary J. Foster, 8 months, died July 10 of flux, daughter
of James and M. J. Foster.

121--George Holsapple, 5 years, 26 days, died Oct. 20, slave of
John Holsapple. Mother was Kate.

122--James Alexander, 64 years, 7 months, died Dec. 11 of parallysis. Born in Monroe County was son of M. and J. Alexander. Death reported by wife, Ingabo Alexander.

123--Catharine Kouns, 52 years, 2 months, 14 days, died Oct. 8
of "dyspepsia." Born in Monroe County, son of George and
M. Kouns. Death reported by M. Kouns, mother.

124--Martha J. Patten, 14, died Nov. 12, daughter of W. and M. J.
Patton (spelled both ways). Reported by William Patton,
uncle.

125--Mary N. Goodall, 16 years, 3 months, 15 days, died Jany. 4
of consumption, daughter of James and Lucy Goodall.

126--Belmira J. Moss, 24, died March 27 of congesion of liver,
daughter of W. R. M. and Nancy Moss.

127--Edmund Meeks died in October, death reported by Mrs. Burditt, acquaintance.

128--James Archer, 80 years, 6 months, death reported by C.
Burns, son-in-law.

129--Susan Foster, 54, died of consumption April 17, wife of
James Foster. Parents were P. and E. Holsapple.

130--James Hogshead, 88 years, 3 months, 21 days, died July 5
of inflamation of bowels. Born in Augusta City, son of
Jno and Anna Hogshead.

131--Miller, slave of Henry W. Moss died July 28.

132--Elizabeth Tegairt, 54 years, died Dec. 9 of bilous cholic.
Born in Pennsylvania, dau. of J. and C. Wickline. Reported
by Jno Hogshead, son-in-law.

133--Frances Baker, 11 years, 5 months (female) died May 6,
daughter of Jno and Nancy Baker.

134--Isaac Caruthers, 82, died Feb. 23 of parallysis. Born
in Rockbridge Co., Va., son of J. and A. Caruthers.
Reported by William Erskine, friend.

135--Martha W. Foster, 4 months, died of croup, daughter of
Geo. W. and Mary Foster.

136--Martha Spangler, 5 months, died March 10 of croup, daughter of S. and E. Spangler.

137--Alice G. Crawford, 10 years, 16 days, died Jan. 3 of
typhoid fever, daughter of J. and N. Crawford.

138--male two-month old of T. N. and E. Burns died March 11
of croup.

139--Mary E. Wiley, 5 months, died May 11, born at Union, daughter of Joseph G. and S. J. Wiley.

140--Thos H. Francis, 15 years, 5 months, 3 days, died June 21
of inflamation of bowels, daughter of Jno E. and E. Francis. Grandmother, Ann Harris, reported death.

141--Martha Clark, 11 years, 8 months, slave of Alexander Clark
died March 7. Born near Union.

142--female, 1 day of F. H. and C. Harris died April 22.

143--Mary E. Gilmer, 31, died of consumption Feb. 20. Born in Louisa Co., Va.
daughter of C. B. and Nancy Terry.
Death reported by Matilda M. Terry,
sister.

144--Nancy Hutchinson, 59 years, 7 months,
15 days, died Sept. 26. Born in Monroe County, daughter of Jno and Rebecca Hutchinson. Death reported by
a brother, John Hutchinson.

Buried in Green Hill Cemetery

in Union

1855

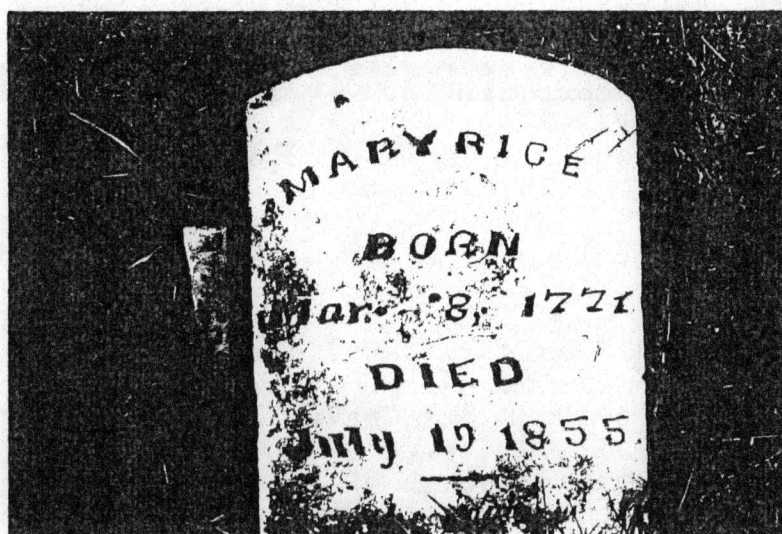

```
        MARY RICE
          BORN
      MARCH 8, 1771
          DIED
      JULY 19, 1855
```

DROPPING LICK CEMETERY

1--Elisha Ewins, 36, died March 24 at Brown's Mill of consumption. Born in Nicholas County, a farmer, wife was
   Mary A. Ewins. Son of M. and P. Ewins.

2--not named son, 5 months old died of fever in April at Wolf
   Creek, son of William and W. Massey.

3--Jonathan Miller, 27 years old, died in June at Dry Run of
   fever and ague. Son of J. and Polly Miller.
   Was laborer.

4--Alex'r J. Erskine, 14, died Feb. 28 at Broad Run of pleurisy.
   Son of A. Erskine.

5--Jas. Y. Scott, 8 days, died of unknown illness at Sinks Oct.
   28, son of G. W. and R. L. Scott.

6--George Watson, 86 years old, died May 25 at Crimson Springs
   of old age. Born in Stafford Co., Va., consort was Nancy
   Watson.

7--not named male, 21 days, died Dec. 1 at Salt Sulphur, son of
   W. and S. Ballard.

8--Oliva W. Counts, 8 months old, died in October at Potts Creek
   of "croop." Parents were Chas. and R. Counts.

9--not named female, 3 days old, died at Salt Sulphur, child of
   Jas. A. and J. F. Porterfield.

10--Anderson Carr, 36 years, died Nov. 2 of white swelling near
    Rocky Point. Son of Sarah Carr.

11--William L. Donally, 1 year, 3 months, 11 days, died Oct. 11
    at Rocky Point of flux.

12--Anna W. Hawkins, 39 years, 8 days, died Aug. 14 near Rocky
    Point of liver complaint. A. M. Hawkins was husband.
    Daughter of Alex'r and Lydia Gray.

13--Mary, 2 years, 3 months, slave of F. Jones and daughter of
    Rhoda Jane, died Sept. 30 near Sinks.

14--Sarah R. Handley, 1 year, 5 months, died Sept. 7 at Sinks
    of flux, daughter of Jas E. and E. E. Handley. Death rep-
    orted by Henrietta Handley, grandmother.

15--Marg't E. B. McLaughlin died March 29 at Rocky Point of
    puerpural fever, no age listed. Born in Pennsylvania,
    death reported by friend, C. H. Burdett.

16--Grean A. McLaughlin, 2 months, died at Rocky Point, son of
    J. G. and M. E. B. McLaughlin. Reported by C. H. Burdett,
    friend.

17--Agness Campbell, 15 years, 6 months, died Sept. 13 at Sinks of flux, daughter of Chas. and E. Campbell. Born in Amherst Co., Va.

18--Alcestra A. Hanger, 7 months, 15 days, died of fever July 15 daughter of D. and E. J. Hanger.

19--Mary, 45, slave of T. Patton, died Feb. 23 at Sinks of fever.

20--Caroline, 20, slave of Richard Dickson, died at Second Creek Nov. 24 of consumption.

21--William P. B. Parkin, 6 years old, died Oct. 9 at Flat Mountain of "dysentery." Son of John A. and E. J. Parkin.

22--not named son, 1 month, 15 days died in July at Beamer's Mill, son of Jas W. and S. Mentz.

23--Jane Charlton, 74, died at Sinks May 7 of old age, daughter of Jos. and F. Ewing. Reported by Jane Charlton, daughter.

24--Martha E. Rye, 2 years, 11 months, 1 day, died April 22 at Sinks of "croop," daughter of W. H. and N. H. Rye.
25--James H. Rye, 9 months, 25 days, died May 27 of "cartarrah fever," son of W. H. and N. H. Rye.

26--Nancy Charton, 28 years, 5 months, 20 days, died Oct. 13 at Sinks. Daughter of J. and L. Parker. Death reported by step-mother, Isabella Parker.

27--Mary Stodgill, 40, died of parallysis at Turkey Creek in June, death reported by A. J. Johnston, brother. Was daughter of R. and M. Johnston.

28--Nancy Cumbee, 87, died of rheumatism Dec. 19 on Peters Mountain. Born in Halifax Co., Va., death reported by a son-in-law, W. M. Sumpter.

29--Adaliza Walker, 38, died at Dropping Lick Dec. 22 of chronic disease. Born in Botetourt Co., Va., daughter of R. and J. Walker. Reported by Henry A. Walker, brother.

30--John Miller, 62, died May 3 at Dropping Lick of disease of the heart, son of Thos. and S. Miller. Born in Monroe County, Sarah Miller was his wife.

31--Mary Campbell, 80, died of old age May 26. Born in Pennsylvania was daughter of Cyrus and Ann Early. Reported by George W. Bland, son-in-law.

32--Margaret Christie, 75, died April 15 at Turkey Creek of pneumonia. Born in Pennsylvania, daughter of A. Crosier. REported by Jas M. Christie, son.

33--Moses Bland, 40, died of consumption at Peters Mountain.
Born in Monroe County, son of A. and S. Bland. Death reported by Alexander Bland, father.

34--Joseph Bland, 44, died of rheumatism on Peters Mountain.
Born in Monroe County, son of Alexander and S. Bland.

35--Henry Jones died West of Turkey Creek of gravel. Was
married. Son of J. and E. Jones.

36--Aaron Morgan died May 9 at Crimson Spring of rheumatism,
son of Ben and Ann Morgan. Born in Lunenburg Co., Va.,
death reported by John E. W. Morgan, son.

37--Joseph Smith, 54, died June 20 on Peters Mountain of dropsy.
Born in Giles Co., Va., son of John and D. Smith. Wife was
Mary Smith.

38--Mary A. Morgan, 11 years, died April 26 at Crimson Spring
of pneumonia, daughter of John E. W. and P. Morgan.

39--Nathan H. Walker, 12 years, 6 months, died Oct. 1 of typhoid
fever at Little Mountain, son of P. G. and Mary Walker. Was
born in Missouri.

40--Jane Gilchris, 78, died July 23 at Back Creek of Cancer.
Born in Scotland. Reported by son Alex' Gilchris.

41--Mary Janie, slave of Andrew Campbell died in September at
Sinks of consumption.

42--George Vass died in June at Swopes Knobs of consumption.
Born in Monroe County, reported by Joseph Dunsmore, son-
in-law.

43--Frances Persinger, 35, died of dropsy Aug. 14 at Sinks,
reported by husband, Jas. Persinger. Born in Greenbrier
County, daughter of Phillip and E. Bowyer.

44--not named male, 9 months old, died June 16 at Flat Top
Mountain of dropsy of brain. Son of James Y. and S. Miller.

45--Rachel B. Waring, 26 years, died Feb. 22 at James Clark's
of puerpural fever. Born in Pennsylvania, death reported
by James Clark, friend.

46--John D. Clark, 30 years, died Nov. 21 of consumption, son
of Jas. and C. Clark.

47--Mary E. McNeigh, 21 years, 6 days, died Dec. 2 at Campbell's
Mill of consumption, daughter of Matthew and N. Campbell.

48--Cornelius, 4 months, slave of Matthew Campbell died in May.

49--Not named male died June 2 near Gap Mills, 2 days old,
    child of G. and Mary C. Mitchell.

50--Sarah F. Counts, 10 years, 5 months, died April 2 at
    Little Devils Creek of not known illness, daughter of
    William and C. Counts.

51--Merekin, 28, slave died in November of Gap of unknown
    illness, owned by Jacob Wickline.

52--Mary A. Eddy, 1 year, 1 month, 1 day died in September of
    flux, child of George W. and S. C. Eddy.

53--Ferdinand N. Piles, 7 months, died of bolt hives June 7
    near Sweet Springs, child of Jacob and W. Piles.

54--Eliza Legg, 1 year, 11 months, 22 days, died Sept. 3 at
    Dunlaps of flux, child of E. P. and L. Legg.

55--Isabella E. Griffith, 9 years, died in September at Dunlaps
    of flux, child of Jefferson and M. Griffith.

56--Richard Howard died at Gap in September, son of G. L. and
    M. Howard. Reported by grandfather, Jacob Bowyer.

57--Sarah C. McGuire, 11 years old, died Sept. 1 at Gap of flux,
    child of Jonathan and J. McGuire. Born in Botetourt Co.,
    Va.

58--Caroly Wickline died Dec. 12 of flux at Gap, child of John
    E. and M. Wickline.

59--Barbra J. R. Hoke, 2 months, 4 days, died Nov. 5 of hives
    at Holsapplis Mountain, child of George W. and M. J. Hoke.

60--Eliza'th Parker, 65, died of dropsy of heart Dec. 13 at
    Parker's Mountain, wife of James Parker. Daughter of William
    and Polly Young.

61--Christopher C. Bostick, 1 year, 1 month, died of flux Sept.
    4 at Cove, child of James L. and M. A. Bostick.

62--Samuel Carlisle, 60, died of flux at Cove Aug. 22. Born in
    Bath County, Va., son of R. and M. Carlisle. Wife was Jane
    Carlisle.

63--Minerva Vance, 23, died on Rich Mountain July 20 of consum-
    ption, death reported by Jacob Vance, father-in-law. Born
    in Monroe County was daughter of R. and H. Reed.

64--Julia H. Dunbar, 36, died of "bed fever" Dec. 25 at Potts
    Creek, wife of J. A. Dunbar. Parents were R. and L. Steele.

65--William Crosier, 71 years, died June 17 at Pott's Creek
of gravel. Born in Pennsylvania was son of A. and E.
Crosier. Sarah Crosier was widow.

66--Margeret Masters, 2 years old, died in November near
Sweet Springs of "hooping cough," child of Frank and R.
Masters.

67--Elizabeth Owens, 61 years old, died May 9 near Sweet Springs
of dropsy, death reported by John Drummond, son-in-law.

68--Oscar, a slave, owned by William Lewis, died near Sweet
Springs of congestion of the brain at age 18 years old.

69--Ellen, a slave, owned by William Lewis, died near Sweet
Springs at age 27 years, was burned to death.

70--Edmund, 53 year-old slave, died near Sweet Springs of pneumonia, owned by William Lewis.

71--Sarah Ann, a slave, owned by Lewis Campbell, died in March
at Union at age 16 years of disease of the heart. Born in
Georgetown, D. C. was daughter of B. and R. Jennings.

72--Simeon Jennings, 74 years, 9 months, 10 days, died Nov. 6
of consumption at Union. Rhoda Jennings was wife.

73--Merit Magann, 50 years, 6 months, died of "quinsey" near
Salt Sulphur on April 4. Born in Bedford Co., Va., was
son of P. and N. Magann. (also spelled Magamn). Wife was
L. E. S. Magann.

74--not named daughter, 3 months, died May 30 at Foot of Knobs
of unknown illness, reported by Allen E. and C. S. Nelson,
parents.

75--William A. Chapman, 9 years, 6 months, died Oct. 6 at Union
of flux, son A. H. and M. Chapman.

76--Caroline Atha, 23, died Dec. 19 of unknown illness, wife
of Lorenzo Atha. Born in Mercer Co., daughter of Robert Vass.

77--John Alderson, 76 years, 10 days, died Sept. 16 of "dispep-
sia." Born in Rockbridge Co., Va. was son of Thos. and Sarah
Alderson. Reproted by Augusta Alderson, daughter.

78--Sarah Jane Ballard, 4 years, 1 months, 16 days, died Feb. 23
of scarlet fever. Born in Monroe County, daughter of Harrison and H. Ballard.

79--Isabel Ballard, 61 years, 9 months, 26 days, died April 8
of "cramp colic." Born in Monroe County, daughter of William E. and Eliz'th Thompson. Willis Ballard, husband.

MONROE COUNTY DEATHS

YEAR OF 1855

80--Anna Bowyer, 58 years, 1 day, died Feb. 5 of consumption.
    Born in Monroe County, John Bowyer, husband, reported the
    death. Was daughter of Polly Blithe.

81--Emily Jane Bobbitt, 4 years, 10 months, 2 days, died Dec.
    25 of asthma, daughter of Oregon and Elizanna Bobbitt. Was
    born in Greenbrier County.

82--Crawford male, one-half day old, died Dec. 18, son of Thomas
    and Nancy Crawford.

83--Anky Canterbury, 42 years, 9 months, 28 days, died Feb. 21
    of unknown illness, daughter of James and Jane Ballard.
    Death reported by father.

84--Dunn female, 4 days old, died March 25 near Pack's Ferry in
    Monroe County, child of John and Polly Dunn.

85--Delilah, slave of Nancy Maddy, died Aug. 12 of consumption
    at age 10 years, 3 months, 9 days. Mother was Mariah.

86--Ellick, slave of John Tiffany, 1 year, 1 months, died May 31
    of unknown illness. Mother was Polly.

87--Eliz'th Foard, 4 years, 7 months, 19 days, died of scarlet
    fever, Jan. 28 at Farms, daughter of Polly Ford.

88--Martha Jane Fulks, 1 year, 7 days, died Sept. 18 of hives,
    child of William and Libby Folks.

89--John Hutchinson, 16 years, 10 months, 17 days, died July 6
    of dropsy of the brain, son of Sam and Cynthia Hutchison.

90--Cornelius Jasper Harless, 8 months, 25 days, died Dec. 8
    at Peterstown of "inflamation of the bowels," son of
    Anthony and Judy Harless.

91--Henry, 3 years, old, died of scarlet fever, slave of John
    Swope. Mother was Betty.

92--John Houchens, 56 years, 5 months, 11 days, died Aug, 31
    in Fayette Co.   of cholera.   Son of John and May Houch-
    ens. Reported by William Houchens, son.

93--John E. Humphreys, 9 years, 3 months, 3 days, died of
    scarlet fever, son of Samuel C. and J. M. Humphreys.

94--Jim, 1 year, 1 month slave of John Swope died of unknown
    illness. Mother was Betty.

95--John, 1 year, 5 months, 20 days, slave of Thomas Johnson
    died of scrofula. Mother was Caroline.

96--Delilah Keatly, 35 years, 11 months, died Aug. 26 of "pain in the head, wife of Joseph Keatly. Parents were Alex and Sarah Hutchison.

97--Sarah C. Meadows, 14 days, died of hives, daughter of jackson and Martha Meadows.

98--Peter McGee died Dec. 14 of cholic, age 1 year, 4 months, 14 days, son of Joel McGhee. Reported by James Evans, grandfather.

99--John A. Miller, 2 years, 1 month, 29 days died of scarlet fever Feb. 22. Son of William and Mary Miller.

100-- Sarah M. Meads, 6 years old, died in May of scarlet fever daughter of William E. and Malinda Meads.

101--James Mann, 68 years, 3 months, 16 days, died Nov. 13 of "strain." Son of Jacob and Mary Mann. Parthena Mann was wife.

102--James McNeer, 40 years, 3 months, 13 days, died Nov. 25 of "remitting fever." Son of Robert and Eliz. McNeer. Wife was Jane McNeer.

103--Stuart McCorkle, 19 years, 1 month, died Sept. 22 of "hemorage of lungs." Son of Samuel and Julie McCorkle.

104--Andrew H. McNeer, 1 year, 7 months, 24 days, died of scarlet fever March 12, son of John and Eliz'th McNeer.

105--Milbon C. Peck, 1 year, 4 months, 22 days, died Aug. 15 of inflamation of brain, son of Green and Margaret Peck.

106--Mary Rice, 82, died of parrallysis July 12, wife of John Rice. Daughter of John and Margaret Sprout.

107--Andrew J. Roach, 14 years, 11 months, 10 days died of scarlet fever, son of James and Polly Roach.

108--James A. Roach, 12 years, 10 months, died of scarlet fever on Nov. 5, son of James and Polly Roach.

109--Martha Ann Ripley, 14 years, 7 months, 26 days, died of consumption July 30, daughte rof Leonard and Anna Ripley.

110--Addison H. Smith, 7 months, 17 days, died of not known illness June 20, son of Ralph and Mary Smith.

111--Agnes Scott, 68 years, 5 months, 29 days, died of asthma March 13, daughter of James and Eliz'th Scott. Reported by James K. Scott, nephew.

112--Fanny Stickler, 39 years, died of consumption Nov. 14, daughter of Lewis and Catherine Stickler. Reported by Jas. Y. Waite, physician.

113--Tabitha Terry, 40 years old, died March 3 of consumption.
     Husband was Jos. Terry. Mother was Elizabeth Pinckley.

114--John Woodrum, 24 years, 1 month, 9 days, died Nov. 3 of
     scrofula, son of John and Judy Woodrum. Reported by John
     Woodrum, father.

115--Warner H. Webb, 37 years, 1 month, 12 days, died Aug. 29
     of scrofula, son of Reuben and Nancy Webb. Reported by
     Fleming Saunders, brother-in-law.

116--Yates male died July 31 of inflamation of brain at age
     1 month, 13 days, son of John and Louisa Yates. Reported
     by John W. yates, father.

ANKEY CANTERBURY
DEC FEB THE 21
        1855
AGE 42 Y. 9 M. 28D

KEATON CEMETERY

1856

Allen Y. Gillam, son of Thos and
Rachel Gillam
Born March 8, 1821
Died Feb. 8, 1856

YEAR OF 1856

1--Peter Miller, 67 years, 3 months, 6 days, died June 12 of
diabetis at Wolf Creek. Jane Miller was wife. Son of V.
and S. Miller.

2--James Erskine, 60 years old, died July 18 at Broad Run of
consumption, son of M. and N. Erskine. Reported by Eleanor
Erskine, wife.

3--Effie A. Rutledge, 1 months, 12 days, died April 6 at Swopes
Knob, cause unknown, daughter of William E. and E. J. Rutledge.

4--Eliza McClowney, 30 years old, died at Turkey Creek of consumption, son of A. and S. Bostick. Husband was Robert Mc-
Clowney.

5--Medora E. Boggess, 8 years old, died Nov. 4 at Dropping Lick
of flux, son of N. and M. A. Boggess.

6--Lewis G. Christie, 9 years, 4 months, died October at Dropping
Lick of flux, son of Thomas M. and C. Christie.
7--William L. Christie, 4 years, 5 months, died in September at
Dropping Lick of flux, son of Thomas M. and C. Christie.

8--William W. Landers, 7 years old, died at Peters Mountain of
flux, son of Jacob and M. J. Landers.

9--Mary, slave of S. C. Campbell died in March at Sinks of old
age.

10--Isaac C. Erskine, 2 months, 27 days, died Jany 25 at Broad
Run of whooping cough, son of John M. and I. J. Erskine.

11--Francis Jones, male, died March 31 at Sinks at age 54 years
of inflamation of the bowels, son of Jas and M. Jones. Wife,
Nancy Jones, reported the death.

12--Not named five-month-old male died Sept. 5 at Rock Point, son
G. and Elizabeth Burwell. Died from inflamation of bowels.

13--Joseph Dunsmore, 80 years old, died March 27 at Sinks of unknown illness, son of J. and E. Dunsmore. Reported by daughter, Elizabeth Dunsmore.

14--Mary Lemons, 78 years old, died of old age Oct. 18 at Sinks,
death reported by son, Abraham Lemons. Born in Augusta Co.,
Va., daughter of J. and E. Carr.

15--Polly Burwell, 77 years old, died Nov. 3 at Sinks of old age,
wife of George Burwell. Born in Augusta Co., Va., daughter of
T. and R. Cunningham.

16--Martha Bostick, 35 years old, died Aug. 1 at Cove Creek of
    unknown illness, wife of Chas. A. Bostick. Born in Monroe
    County, daughter of J. and E. Parker.

17--Reuben Bostick, 45 years old, died Dec. 18 of small pox,
    son of J. and E. Bostick. Death reported by Jas Parker,
    father-in-law.

18--Martha Bostick, 21 years old, died Dec. 8 of small pox,
    daughter of R. and M. Bostick. Death reported by Jas. Par-
    ker, grandfather.

19--Not named male died Oct. 6 at Sinks, child of Thos F. and M.
    A. Nickell.

20--Paulina Tomlinson, 26 years old, died May 27 at Sinks of
    dropsy, daughte rof D. and Sarah Tomlinson. Born in Amherst
    County, Va.

21--Lucy Humphreys, 32 years, 5 months, died March 4 at Sinks of
    consumption, death reported by Sarah Tomlinson, mother. Born
    in Amherst Co., Va., daughter of D. and S. Tomlinson.

22--Calvin Moss, 3 years old, died of croop, son of Henry and N.
    Moss.

23--Andrew Summers, 50 years, 4 months, died Aug. 26 at Gap Mills
    of remetting fever. Born in Augusta Co., Va., wife was Olivia
    Summers. Parents were A. and M. Summers.

24--Martha J. Mentz, 1 year, 10 months, 25 days, died March 30
    at Cove Creek, child of Robert C. L. and S. J. Mentz. Born in
    Alleghany Co., Va.

25--John Neel, 78 years old, died Oct. 1 at Back Creek of flux,
    son of O. and J. Neel. Wife was Mary Neel.

26--Owen W. Chrisman, 5 years, 4 months, died Oct. 16 at Gap of
    flux, son of F. and Mary Chrisman.

27--Lucinda E. McCommack, 8 years, 10 months, died Sept. 17 at
    Gap of flux, daughter of J. and E. W. McCommack.

28--Ruth McNutt, 86 years, 6 months, died Aug. 27 at Gap of dro-
    psy. Born in Prince William Co., Va., daughter of F. and E.
    Legg. Death reported by Robert McNutt, son.

29--Mary, 6 years, 11 months, 29 days, slave owned by Ingabo
    Alexander, and daughter of Mariah, died July 29 at Gap of
    flux.

30--Kelton Eads died May 2 of dropsy, reported by Ben Burns,
    son-in-law.

31--Emma Neel, 2 months 15 days, died Sept. 27 at Gap of unknown illness, child of William and M. Neel.

32--Nancy M. Burns, 11 months, 27 days, died Oct. 23 at Laurel Creek of sore throat, daughter of Andrew and M. A. Burns.

33--Sarah C. Howell, 51 years old, died in November near Union of dropsey in chest. Born in Augusta Co., Va., daughter of T. and L. Davis. Death reported by Jas C. Clark, brother-in-law.

34--Mary, 20 years old, slave of S. P. Holsapple, died Feb. 25 at Dutch Corner of white swelling, reported by Phillip Holsapple.

35--James A. Higginbotham, 4 years, 10 days, died in March at Laurel Creek, son of A. W. and S. A. Higginbotham.

36--not named male died at Union, son of L. and M. A. Campbell.

37--Rachel Bean, 66 years, 7 months, died Nov. 7 at Potts Creek of paralysis. Born in Rockbridge Co., Va., daughter of J. and E. Wiseman. Husband was William Been.

38--Nancy Been, 41 years, 7 months, died Oct. 11 at Potts Creek of fever, daughter of W. and R. Been.

39--Andrew Bastin, 3 months old, slave of William Been, died of whooping cough at Potts Creek.

40--James H. McCartney, 49 years, 5 months, died June 26 at Sweet Springs of consumption, husband of Isabell McCartney. A carpenter, born in Botetourt Co., Va., son of J. and J. McCartney.

41--Lewis, 17 years old, slave of Francis Dunlap, died at Union of consumption.

42--Jane M. Boyd, 50 years, 5 months, 5 days, died Aug. 8 at Union of cancer of the womb. Born in Greenbrier County, daughter of J. and E. Dunnevant. Death reported by Oliver P. Nelson, son-in-law.

43--David Hutcheson, 73 years old, died March 26 at Union of old age. Born in Augusta Co., Va., death reported by John T. Fegget, son-in-law.

44--John Francis, 93 years old, 1 month, died Dec. 29 at Knobs of old age. Born in Cecil Co., Md., son of George and Jane Francis. Death reported by Rebecca Francis, daughter.

45--Isabell Francis, 91 year, 1 month, 21 days, died March 15
     of old age at Knobs. Born in Cecil Co., Md., daughter of
     H. and J. Erskine. Death reported by Rebecca Francis,
     daughter.

46--John Robertson, 78 years old, died of chronic rheumatism
     at Union, son of T. and B. Robertson. Was born in Scotland.
     Death reported by Walter Douglas, a friend.

JOHN ROBERTSON

BORN

MAY 15, 1777

IN DALMONNY, SCOTLAND

DIED NOV. 5th 1856

AT UNION, VA.

TOMBSTONE BY:
GADDESS
LYNCHBURG, VA.

BURIED IN GREEN HILL CEMETERY AT UNION

MONROE COUNTY DEATHS

YEAR OF 1856

1--Elizabeth Virginia Saunders, 3 months, 17 days, died Jany.
   7 of "bronchitus" child of Jackson P. and Elizabeth A. Saunders.

2--Bird Clark, 5 years, 6 months, 5 days, died July 16 of bronchitis, son of Armstrong and Nancy Woodram.

3--William Fleshman, 30 years, 2 months, died Dec. 9 of consumption, son of John and Nancy Fleshman. Unmarried, death reported by Col. F. Fleshman, brother.

4--Felix Williams, 90 years, 3 days, died June 9 of dropsey. Born
   in Orange Co., Va., wife was Nancy Williams. Was son of Francis Williams. Death reproted by Felix Williams, son.

5--Sarah Comer Tuggle, 3 months, 28 days, died June 20, daughter
   of Lewis and Emilly Tuggle. Death reported by Larkin Tuggle,
   grandfather.

6--Archibald Swinney McGee, 5 months, 30 days, died April 13, son
   of Jas. and Cintha McGhee.

7--27-day-old son of Joseph and Mary Phillips died Oct. 28.

8--James William Ellison, 20 days died Jany. 16 of croup, son of
   Samuel and Ann Ellison.

9--Joseph Haynes, 1 year, 2 months, 19 days, died Aug. 8, son of
   Alex'n and Jane Haynes. Reported by James Dunlap, relation.

10--Oliver Fulton, 45 years, slave of Frances Dunlap, died Sept.
    29. Reported by James Dunlap.

11--Nancy Jane Brown, 19 year, 7 months, 12 days, died May 24 of
    measles, daughter of Anderson and Agnes Brown. Unmarried.

12--Rebecca Susan Pine, 8 years, 7 months, 23 days, died Oct. 13
    of flux, daughter of Madison and Mahala Pine.

13--Rachael Riffe, 62 years, 4 months, 13 days, died Oct. 13
    Born in Albermarle Co., Va., was daughter of David and Cath-
    arine Riffe.

14--Samuel, 9 years old, slave of John Swope died Oct. 28 of
    flux.

15--Willis, 45 years old, salve of William Smith, died Feb. 12
    of broken limb.

16--William Henderson Foster, 3 years, 4 months, 27 days, son
    of Jas. and Nancy Foster, died May 23.

17--Walter H. Riddle, 8 months, 20 days, died Sept. 5 of hives,
    son of John and Martha Riddle.

18--Thomas Jefferson Fry, 28 days, son of Isaac and Sarah Fry, died May 3.

19--William Alexander Fry, 15 yerars, 10 months, 2 days, died May 7 of scrofula, son of Isaac and Margaret Fry.

20--Clementine V. Gibson, 19 years, 11 months, 12 days, died April 20 of consumption, wife of Adam Gibson. Daughter of Jas. and Nancy Mann. Reported by Lewis J. Mann, brother.

21--Archibald, 24 years old, slave of Shannon Butt, died Dec. 15 of inflamation of liver.

22--Mary Herron, 34 years, 6 months, 2 days, died Oct. 28 of consumption, daughter of Harry Payne.

23--Sarah Ann Hinton, 3 years, 1 month, 29 days, died Feb. 13 was scalded, daughter of Peter and Eliza Hinton.

24--Male child of William G. and Amarida C. Woodram died in December, no age listed.

25--Samuel McCorkle, 42 years, 6 months, 17 days, died of consumption, husband of Julia McCorkle. Born in Greenbrier Co., was son of Saml. and Eliz. McCorkle. Was farmer.

26--Amanda R. Thomas, 2 months, 27 days, died Nov. 3, daughter of Santy and S. Graham.

27--Elizabeth Lowe, 56 years, 6 months, 29 days, died Oct. 28 of typhoid fever, wife of Mathur Lowe. Born in Monroe County, daughter of Ralph and Eliz. Clark.

28--One day old child of James and Malinda Meadows died Oct. 21.

29--One-day-old child of Richard and Mary Wiseman died June 11.

30--Jane Pack, 76 years, 2 months, 6 days, died Jan. 19 of dropsy. Born in Greenbrier County, daughter of William Hutchison. Husband was John Pack. Death reported by Archivald Pack, son.

31--Joseph A. Upton, 53 years, 7 months, 15 days, died May 29 of consumption, son of Loyd and Nancy Upton. Born in Monroe County, wife was Mary Upton.

32--Jacob Ellis, 78 years, 7 months, 19 days, died Oct. 14 of old age, husband of Margaret Ellis. Born in Augustua Co., Va., was son of Owen and C. Ellis. Death reported by G. Ellis, son.

MONROE COUNTY DEATHS

YEAR OF 1856

33--Elizabeth Allen, 71 years, 10
    months, 22 days, died Dec. 9
    of dropsy. Born in Monroe Co-
    unty, was daughter of Jas.
    and Sarah Christie. Husband
    was Andrew Allen. Death was
    reported by Jas W. Johnson,
    son-in-law.

            BURIED IN GREEN HILL
                 CEMETERY

            AT UNION

34--Eliza Angelin Perry, 1 year, 11 months, 26 days, died
    Nov. 7 of croup, daughter of George and Nancy Perry.

35--Louisa Bowyer, 15 years, 1 month, 7 days, died Oct. 12
    daughter of John and P. Bowyer.

36--Rachel Helms, 44 years, died April 25 of dropsy, wife
    of Adam Helms. Death reported by a son, Andrew Helms.
    Daughter of William and Alcey Sulfin. (Sutfin?)

            ****

1857

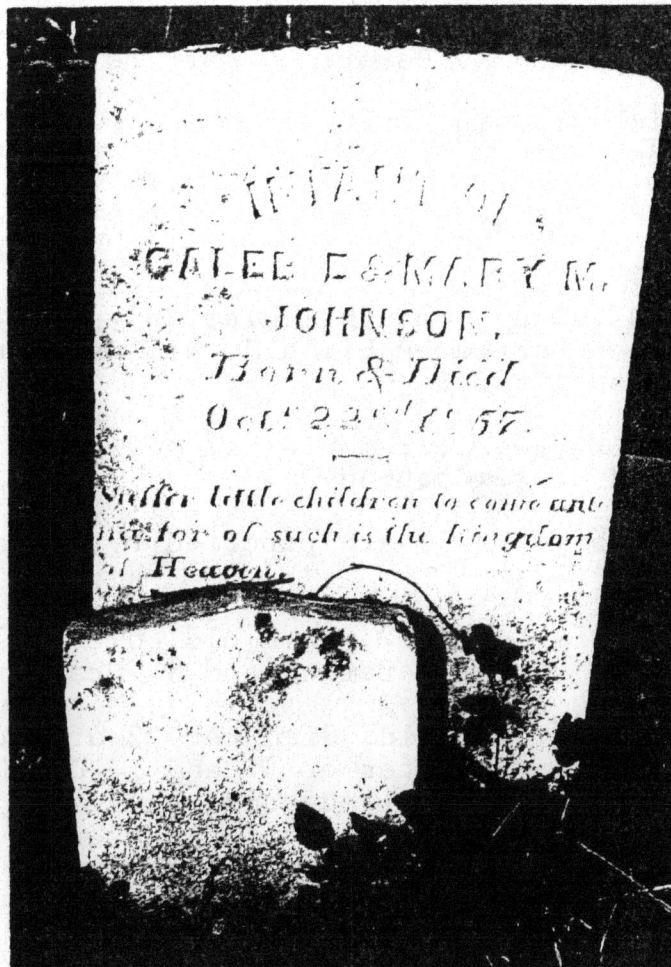

INFANT OF CALEB E. AND

MARY M. JOHNSON

ON WOLF CREEK

MONROE COUNTY DEATHS

YEAR OF 1857

1--Michael Alexander, 78 years old, died Jany. 29 of unknown
   illness. Born in Monroe Co., son of J. and I. Alexander.
   Was married. Death reported by son, Jno E. Alexander.

2--Jessee, 39 years old, slave of Ingabo Alexander died Sept.
   23 of penumonia. Born in Greenbrier County.

3--Robert Bland, 73 years old, died Oct. 22 "cause of death
   not ascertained." Born in Monroe County, son of R. and A.
   Bland. Married. Death reported by George W. Bland, son.

4--Jacob G. Baker, 17 years, 3 months, died Nov. 20 of typhoid
   fever, son of Jno and N. Baker. Unmarried.

5--James E. Bostick died in February of unknown illness, son of
   _____ and M. Bostick. Death reported by wife, E. S. Bostick.

6--Virinda C. Been, 2 years, 8 months, 27 days, died Jany. 21
   of worm fever, daughter of William M. and M. Been.

7--Nathan Boyd, 60 years, 5 months, died July 10 of consumption.
   A tailer, death reported by Eliza J. Nelson, daughter. Son
   of Jas and Florence Boyd.

8--Henley Chapman, 21 years, 2 months, 7 days, died June 18,
   son of A. A. and M. R. Chapman.

9--Eliza Cummels, 45 years, death reported by William F. Sydnor,
   friend.

10--Jeremiah W. C. Crawford, 17 years old, died July 13 of con-
   jestion of brain, son of Jeremiah and N. Crawford.

11--Rebecca Clark, 60 years old, died Feby 2 of apoplexy. Born
   in Augusta Co., Va., daughter of J. and I. Dickey. Death
   reported by Alexander Clark, husband.

12--Samuel Clark, 93 years, 8 months, died Jany 20 of "infirmity."
   Born in Augusta Co., Va. Death reported by James Clark, son.

13--Elizabeth Clark, 67 years old, died May 13 of consumption,
   wife of John Clark. Born in Pennsylvania, daughter of Thos.
   and M. Johnston.

14--William A. Campbell, 10 years, 1 month, 5 days, died Feb. 8
   of inflamation of brain, son of C. B. and S. Campbell.

15--John Dickson, 77 years old, died Feby 21 of bronchitis. Born
   in Greenbrier County, was a tailor, son of Jos. and L. Dickson. Reported by Thos E. Dickson, son.

16--Mary H. Dickson, 19 years, 8 months, 19 days, died Jany 31 of "puerpural fever." Born in Monroe County, daughter of S. and S. Hamilton. Death reported by Elizabeth Dickson, mother-in-law.

17--Mary, 44-year-old slave of Richard Dickson died May 2 of consumption.

18--Susan Duncan, 32, died April 6 of "puerpural fever, wife of William L. Duncan. Born in Montgomery Co., Va., daughter of G. and S. Miller.

19--Augustus Erskine, 31 years, 11 months, died in March of unknown illness. Born in Monroe County, son of ____ and Betsy Erskine. Reported by Margaret Scott, friend.

20--Charles A. Erskine, 3 months, 28 days, died March 17, son of J. M. and I. J. Erskine.

21--Alexander E. Fullen, 8 years, 11 months, 22 days, died Jany 21 "by a fall." Son of Jno. and C. Fullen.

22--Thompson R. Goodall, 35 years, 3 months, 13 days, died May 10 of consumption. Born in Orange County, Va., son of J. and S. Goodall. Reported by wife, Mary A. Goodall.

23--Sarah F. Hutchinson, 31 years, 11 months, 23 days, died April 22 of consumption. Born in Alleghany Co., Va., daughter of Jno. and A. Crow. Reported by George W. Hutchinson, husband.

24--Not named child of William and M. J. Hall died Feb. 5 of unknown illness, 1 day old.

25--Jane Hogshead, 75 years old, died May 19 of "constriction of bowels." Born in Augusta Co., Va., daughter of J. and E. McGlamory. Reported by son, Humphrey Hogshead.

26--John Hogshead, 50 years, 11 months, 23 days, died July 7 of inflamation of bowels.

27--Elizabeth Holms, 57 years old, died Oct. 21 of consumption. Death reported by Lewis A. Holms, son. Born in Greenbrier County, daughter of A. and M. Burdett.

28--John Hull, 68 years, died May 28 of "dropsey in chest," son of H. and E. Hull. Born in Augusta Co., Va. Death reported by Sophia Hull, wife.

29--Martha Huffman, 23 years, died in September of unknown illness, wife of A. Huffman. Born in Monroe County, daughter of H. and E. Jones.

30--Jas. A. Jeffreys, 23 years, 25 days, died July 29 of consumption, son of J. and H. A. Jeffreys. Reported by S. J.
   Jeffreys, wife.

31--Robert Mentz, 76 years old, died in October of inflamation
   of bowels. Born in Rockbridge Co., Va., parents unknown.
   Reported by Jas W. Mentz, son.

32--Jennetta Morris, 20 years old, died July 10 of consumption,
   daughter of Nathan and J. Morris.

33--Nancy A. Morris, 19 years, died Aug. 13 of "puerpural fever,'
   daughter of A. and S. Eads. Was married. Death reported by
   Jno Neighbors, step-father.

34--Margaret A. H. Patton, 21 years, died June 3 of consumption,
   daughter of Tristrem and E. E. Patton.

35--14-day-old not named son of Susanna, slave died Jany. 22.
   Owned by Tristrem Patton.

36--Jas. L. Prentice, 38 years old, died Dec. 17 of consumption.
   Son of M. and E. Prentice. Reported by Elizabeth Prentice,
   sister. Was married.

37--John Reaburn, 81 years old, died Sept. 27 of hemmorrhage,
   son of J. and E. Reaburn. Unmarried. Death reported by
   George W. Reaburn, nephew.

38--Mary Reaburn, 75 years, 3 months, 23 days, died March 18 of
   pulmonary disease. Born in Augusta Co., Va., daughter of
   William and P. Hamilton. Death reported by Charles Reaburn,
   husband.

39--Mary Spade, 84 years old died Sept. 21 of old age. Born in
   Switzerland, was a widow. Death reported by Samuel Dehart,
   son-in-law.

40--Lucy, 35 year old slave of Fanny Dunlap, died in October of
   unknown illness.

41--John Scott, 74 years old, died May 24 of unknown illness,
   son of J. and E. Scott. Born in Monroe County, death reported by Matthew Scott, brother.

42--Elizabeth Steele, 83 years, 1 month, died in February of a
   cold. Born in Bath Co., Va., daughter of R. and E. Armstrong. Reported by Matilda Perry, daughter.

43--James Steele, 82 years old, died in November of unknown
   illness. Born in North Carolina was married. Death reported by daughter, Matilda Perry.

44--David Tomlinson, 61 years, 10 months, 21 days, died Aug. 18
  of unknown illness. Born in Amherst Co., Va., son of A. and
  M. Tomlinson. Death reported by Sarah Tomlinson, wife.

45--Sarah Wickline, 42 years old, died Aug. 27 of cancer. Born
  in Monroe County, daughter of W. and M. Neel. Death reported by husband, W. Wickline.

46--Cornelius, 2 years old, owned by James S. Woodville, died
  of convulsions.

YEAR OF 1857

1--Leonard Turner, 76 years old, died July 17 near Forest Hill
  of paulsy. Born in Eastern Virginia, wife was Matilda Turner. Reported by son, Preston Turner.

2--Male child of Charles and Augustus Humphreys died July 20
  at Willis Tinsley's home of "not known" illness. Willis
  Tinsley was grandfather.

3--Salina Saunders, 23 years, 8 months, 2 days, died May 20 on
  Wolf Creek Mountain of "quinsey." Wife of R. W. Saunders,
  Sr. Born in Monroe County, daughter of Isaac and Mary Mil-
  burn.

4--Martha Hutchison, 29 years, 1 month, 5 days, died Feby 26
  at Forest Hill, wife of B. B. Hutchison. Born in Monroe Co.,
  daughter of William and Barbara Hines.

5--Joel R. Holden, 6 months, 3 days, died Sept. 30 of "not known"
  illness, son of Smith and Mary Holden.

6--Edith Boggess, 72 years, 1 day, died Feby 5 on Wolf Creek Mt.,
  of cancer, daughter of Rachel Wiseman. Wife of Seth Boggess.
  Death reported by William Smith, relation.

7--Mary A. Goodall, 2 years, 1 month, 9 days, died Dec. 20 on
  Chestnut Hill, daughter of William and Virginia Goodall.

8--Allen M. Bassham, 28 years, 4 months, 1 day, died Oct. 11
  on Chestnut Hill, son of Jno. and Catharine Bassham. Wife
  was Margaret Bassham. Death reported by father.

9--Luanaa, 30 years old, slave of Jno Riddle, died Nov. 13 near
  Red Sulphur of disease of lungs.

10--Lucy Broyles, 63 years, died Sept. 4 in Valley of "not known" illness. Born in Madison Co., Va., daughter of Jno.
  and Lydia Riner. Absalem Broyles, husband.

11--Mary Syms, 22 years, 9 months, 17 days, died May 7 of consumption, daughter of Jno. and E. Syms. Reported by Lewis
  Syms, brother.

12--two-day-old child of Andy and Sarah Broyles died in May at
    "Hands" Creek of not known illness.

13--Elizabeth Mitchell, 48 years, 11 months, 23 days, died Oct.
    18 near "Hands" Creek of not known illness, born Eastern Va.,
    daughter Massy Patteson. Wife of Joseph Mitchell.

14--William L. Mitchell, 1 year, 8 months, 29 days, died May
    30, was "scalded." Son of Lewis and Mary Mitchell.

15--Margaret G. Mitchell, 3 years, 4 months, 26 days, died Sept.
    15 of flux, son of Lewis and Mary Mitchell.

16--Mary E. Mitchell, 6 years, 3 months, 12 days, died Sept. 22
    of flux, daughter of Lewis and Mary Mitchell.

17--Dorothy Harvey, 71 years, 9 months, 33 days, died Dec. 6 at
    Flat Woods of cancer. Born in Louisa Co., Va., daughter of
    Jas. and Mary Gentry. Wife of Rich'd Harvey.

18--Mary R. Humphreys, 4 years, 7 months, 23 days, died Oct. 4
    at Centerville of flux, daughter of Alex'd J. and E. Humph-
    reys. Born in Bath Co., Va.

19--Manerva Humphreys, 3 years, 11 months, 21 days, died Oct.
    22 at Centerville of flux, daughter of Alex' J. and E. Hum-
    phreys. Born in Monroe County.

20--Robert Willey, 6 years old, died June 5 at Indian Creek of
    fever, child of Eber and Judy Willey.

21--John Mann, 5 years, 6 months, 11 days, died Oct. 10 at "Hands"
    Creek of fever, son of A. and E. Mann.
22--Martha Mann, 7 years, 3 months, 20 days, died Oct. 10 at Hands
    Creek of fever, daughter of Arch'd and E. Mann.

23--Ananias Meadow, 2 years, 8 months, 30 days, died Dec. 27 at
    White Tree Hill of croup, child of Sparrel and Mary Meader.
    Born in Roanoke Co., Va.

24--Elizabeth Baber, 61 years, 9 months, 12 days, died Feb. 16
    near Red Sulphur of not known illness. Born in Amherst Co.,
    Va., daughter of Kellis and Mary Tuning. Husband was James
    Baber.

25--Winslow Ballard, 47 years, 7 months, 18 days, died April 9
    on Waters of Indian Creek , husband of Sarah Ballard. Born
    in Monroe County, son of William and Polly Ballard.

26--Jas. L. Bostick, 30 years, 5 months, 30 days, died March
    18 on Wiseman Mountain of consumption, husband of Margaret
    Bostick. Son of Arch'd and Sarah Bostick. Father repor-
    ted death.

27--Jacob Smith, 2 years, 2 months, 14 days, died April 1 at
Indian Creek of flux, son of Jackson and C. Smith.

28--Millard F. Smith, 6 years, 11 months, 24 days, died April
18 at Indian Creek of flux, son of Jackson and C. Smith.

29--Mary A. Haynes, 9 months, 17 days, died Dec. 30 at R. V.
Shanklin's of "not known illness," son of Alex'r and Jane
Haynes. R. V. Shanklin, grandfather, reported death.

30--Polly E. Miller, 6 years, 4 months, 6 days, died Sept. 19
at Springfield of flux, daughter of Rufus and Mary Miller.

31--Jas. M. Fry, 5 years, 11 months, 4 days, died June 3 at
Centerville of scrofula, son of Isaac and Margaret Fry.

32--Ann E. Fry, 3 years, 2 months, 16 days, died Nov. 16 at
Centerville of scrofula, daughter of Isaac and Margaret
Fry.

33--Jno W. Taylor, 8 months, 23 days, died Oct. 20 at Indian
Creek of fever, son of Henry and M. E. Taylor.

34--Agness Kerby, 8 months old died in August near Cross Roads,
daughter of William and Mary Kerby.

35--Isaac Painter, 56 years, 1 month, died April 18 at Alderson's Ferry of consumption, son of J. and E. Painter. Death reported by Sarah Painter, wife.

36--Robert Syms, 80 years, 7 months, 10 days, died July 28 at
Wolf Creek Mountain of scrofula. Born in Virginia, son of
Jerry Syms. Sarah Syms was wife. Death reported by son,
John Syms.

37--Elizabeth Johnson, 31 years, died Dec. 23 near Rollinsburg
of consumption. Born in Giles County, daughter of Rueben
and E. Johnson. Death reported by father.

38--Sarah A. Stevens, 19 years, 4 months, 3 days, died April
19 at Kelly's Creek of consumption. Born in Monroe Co.,
daughter of Jeremiah and Miram Stevens.

39--Jno J. Huffman, 9 months, 17 days, died July 8 at Stoney
Creek of "neumonia." Son of Samuel and S. J. Huffman Jr.

40--Joseph Graham, 81 years, 2 months, 19 days, died Dec. 8
at Keeny's Knob of inflamation of liver. Born in Augusta
Co., Va., son of David and Jane Graham. Wife was Rebecca
Graham. Death reported by Jno Graham, son.

41--Elizabeth Ballenger, 41 years, 5 months, 30 days, died
Jany. 12 of dropsy at Kenny's Knob, daughter of Joseph
and Rebecca Graham. Wife of Arch'd Ballenger.

42--Malinda <u>Nettle</u>, 13 years, 2 months, 12 days, died Nov. 8
near Peterstown of quinsey.

43--William <u>Nettle,</u> 6 years, 3 months, 24 days, died Nov. 9
near Peterstown of quinsey.

44--Brown L. <u>Nettle</u>, 10 years, 9 months, 25 days, died Nov.
19 near Peterstown of quinsey.
All were children of Abram and Lucy Nettle.

45--Alex'r D. <u>Haynes</u>, 33 years, 9 months, 13 days, died Nov.
14 at Red Sulphur of typhoid fever. A merchant, was son
of J. M. and Isabella Haynes. Wife was Jane Haynes. Death
reported by mother, Isabella Haynes.

46--Rebecca <u>Carden</u>, 40 years, 9 months, 13 days, died May 1
on Greenbrier River of not known illness. Husband was
Isaac Carden, who reported the death. Daughter of Alexander and Sarah Hutchison.

9	Huffman Martha	W		Unknown	23	
30	Jeffreys Jas A	W		Consumption	23	2c
1	Maxley Robert	W		Infn of Bowels	76	
2	Manis Jennette	W		Consumption	20	
3	" Nancy A	W		Puerperal fever	19	
4	Patten Margaret A M	W		Consumption	21	
5	Not Named	W		Unknown		14
6	Prentice Jas L	W		Consumption	38	
7	Realan John	W		Hemmorrhage	81	
8	" Mary	W		Pulmonary disease	75 3	23
9	Spade Mary	W		Old age	54	
10	Lucy	S Fanny Dunlap	Unknown	35	
1	Scott John	W		"	74	
2	Steece Elizabeth	W		Cold	83 1	
3	" James	W		Unknown	82	
4	Tomlinson David	W		"	61 10 21	
5	Wickline Sarah	W		Cancer	42	
6	Cornelius	S Jas S Woodrall	Convulsions	2	

1858

FIELDEN MEADOWS

DIED 1858

BURIED IN PETERSTOWN CEMETERY

MONROE COUNTY DEATHS

YEAR OF 1858

1--Nancy Landers, 96 years old, died Oct. 10, was widow and "pentioner." Death reported by son, Jacob Landers.

2--female slave of George Moss died Oct. 20 at Gap Mills, was 60 years, 10 months and 5 days old. Born in Monroe County.

3--Thomas H. Dunbar, 2 years, 7 months, 1 day, died Oct. 11 near Gap Mills of flux, son of John A. V. and Mary Elizabeth Dunbar.

4--Susannah Young, 87 years, 11 months, 29 days, widow, died of old age March 2 near Rocky Point. Death reported by Susan C. Young, daughter.

5--Joseph Fisher, 70 years old, died Dec. 13 near Rocky Point of "rheumaticks." Agness Fisher was consort.

6--Margaret Dunsmore, 71 year, 6 months, died Sept. 20 near Rocky Point of unknown illness. Wife of James Dunsmore.

7--James Lewis Earley, 9 year, 10 months, 6 days, died March 12 of flux, son of William and Hannh Earley.

8--Catharine Boyd, 21 years, 11 months, 2 days, died May 9 on Knob of consumption, daughter of Robert and Catharine Boyd.

9--No name male, 2 days old, died May 9, child of John Lilly and Rebecca Shirer.

10--Joshua Leach, 85 years, 7 months, 27 days, died Oct. 9 in Sinks of old age. Was a widower. Son, Edmund Leach, reported the death.

11--William, slave of William Been, 25 years, 5 months, 10 days, died at Potts Creek April 25 of "bil."

12--Polly Carpenter, 45 years, 8 months, died Feb. 28 of consumption of lung. Single, daughter of Nathan and Susannah Carpenter. Death reported by J. W. Carpenter, brother.

13--Clarah Shiree, 70 years old, died at Gap Valley of "parilises," reported by John Shiree, husband.

14--Lyddy Moss, 69 years, 5 months, 16 days, died Aug, 31 near Sweet Springs, reported by George Moss, husband.

15--Thomas Floid Reynolds, 2 years, 8 months, died Aug, 15 at Sinks of flux, son of Frances and Mariah Reynolds.

16--Christopher C. Reynolds, 4 months old died Dec. 28 at Sinks of flux, son of Frances and Mariah Reynolds.

17--Joseph Perry Charlton, 38 years, 5 months, 6 days, died
    at Sinks of cancer, son of Joseph Charlton. Wife was
    Liddy C. Charlton. Reported by Thomas Charlton, brother.

18--Betsy, 6 months, 2 days, slave of Andrew Gray died Oct.
    10 near Union of "feaver."

19--Three years, 2 months old slave (male) of Andrew Gray
    died Oct. 2 near Union of fever.

20--Mary Ann Long, 27 years, 9 months, 8 days, died May 25
    near Union of consumption of lungs, daughter of Jacob and
    Sarah Long. Was single.

21--Female child of Jas. A. and Susannah Homes died March 29 at
    Sinks of unknown illness.

22--Female child of Jos. F. and Margarell Ann Cook died Aug. 29
    in Monroe of unknown illness.

23--Ellen Marthy Foster, 28 years, 2 months, 10 days, died Oct.
    25 of consumption of lungs, wife of Etty Milton Foster.

24--Thomas McCaleb , 76 years, 2 months, 20 days, died July 12
    of "gravel," husband of Sarah McCaleb. Born in Bedford Co.
    Va., was a wagon maker. Death reported by Robert B. McCaleb,
    son.

25--Polly Neel , 69 years, 1 months, 3 days, died Dec. 20 of
    "parilises." Husband was William H. Neel. Death reported
    by a neighbor, Thomas E. Dickson.

26--Adline Burns, 28 years, 4 months, died of consumption of
    the lungs. Death reported by Christopher Burns, brother.

27--Three-month, 3 day-old daughter of Joseph L. Carlisle
    died July 20.

28--Elisabeth Tailor, 58 years, died June 3 of "not known"
    illness. Was a widow. Death reported by son, William C.
    Tailor.

YEAR OF 1858

1--William T. Akers died at Peterstown of tyfoid fever. Was
   a merchant.

2--William Buckland, 31 years, 3 months, died June 21 at Peterstown, husband of Cynthia Buckland. Son of Jno and Mary
   Buckland. Death reported by Jacob Buckland, brother.

3--Sarah Broyles, 18 years, 7 months, 21 days, died Dec. 22
    at Brier Run of consumption, wife of Solomon Broyles. Rep-
    orted by Augustus Broyles, son.

4--Lewis C. Ballard, 8 years, 9 months, 8 days, died Aug. 28
    at Stinking Lick of flux, son of Silvester and Lucinda.

5--Catharine Ballard, 11 year, 9 months, 4 days, died Sept.
    24 at Stinking Lick of flux, daughter of William F. and
    Eliza Ballard.

6--Jno H. Cawley, 3 months old, died June 10 at Chestnut Hill
    of hives, son of Jas. L. A. and Elizabeth Cawley.

7--Perliena Chambers, 59 years, 10 months, 2 days, died April
    8 at Peterstown of "tyfoid" fever. Born in Albermarle Co.,
    Va., daughter of William and Mary Ballard. William F. Cham-
    bers, husband.

8--George Caldwell, 23 years old, died Feby. 8 at Peterstown
    of "tyfoid" fever. Born in Giles County, son of Jas T. Cald-
    well. Single, death reported by P. H. Spangler, friend.

9--Elizabeth Callaway, 57 years, 10 months died July 9 near Pet-
    erstown of "tyfoid" fever, wife of Vincent Callaway. Born in
    Bath Co., Va., daughter of William Thompson.

10--Nancy J. Craft 7 months, 7 days, died Nov. 3 on Greenbrier
    River of unknown illness, daughter of Jas. and Ursula Craft.

11--David W. Diddle, 32 years, died March 30 at Peterstown of
    tyfoid fever, son of D. and Catharine Diddle. Wife was E. L.
    Diddle. Reported by William F. Chambers, relation.

12--Eliza J. Dunn, 10 years, 17 days, died July 21 at Rich Creek
    of flux, daughter of Joseph and Eliz Dunn.

13--Hugh Dillion, 1 month, 7 days, died Aug. 16 of flux, son of
    Wright and Eliz Dillion.

14--Jno Dunn Sr., 52 years, 11 months, 12 days, died May 5 of
    "tyfoid fiver" at Rich Creek. Son of John and Mary Dunn.
    Death reported by John M. Dunn, son.

15--Delila Dunn, 13 years, 9 months, 25 days, died May 5 at
    Rich Creek of "tyfoid" fever, daughter of John and Agness
    Dunn. Death reported by John M. Dunn, brother.

16--John F. Dunn, 28 years, 8 months, 13 days, died Jan. 9
    at Rich Creek of tyfoid fever, son of James and Nancy Dunn.
    Death reported by father.

17--Henry A. Dillion, 1 year, 11 months 29 days, died at
   Rich Creek of flux, son of Anslum and Louisa Dillion.
18--William N. Dillion, 6 years old, died at Rich Creek of
   flux, son of Anslum and Louisa Dillion.

19--Christopher Dillion, 18 years, died at Rich Creek of
   typhoid fever July 29, son of John and Martha Dillion.

20--Luther H. Dunn, 1 year-old, died July 25 of flux, son of
   Harrison and Martha Dunn.

21--Mahala J. Furgerson, 1 year old died June 23 of flux, daughter of Eli and Cath' Furgerson.

22--Wiley Furgerson, 31 years, died June 20 of typhoid fever,
   husband of M. Furgerson. Born in Franklin Co., Va., son of
   John and Ann Furgerson. Death reported by James Meadows.

23--Dr. Thomas Fowler, 59 years, died of congestion of the brain,
   April 2 at Indian Creek. Born in Tennessee, was a physician
   and son of Thomas and Mary Fowler. Wife was Priscilla
   Fowler.

24--Warlopa, (Indian), 10 years old died at Indian Creek of unknown illness. Born in California, death reported by Dr.
   R. A. Pearis.

25--Samuel C. Gwinn, 7 years old, died Aug. 8 of flux, son of
   Samuel and Sarah Gwinn.
26--Joseph L. Gwinn, 5 years old, died Aug. 13 of flux, son of
   Samuel and Sarah Gwinn.

27--Rachel Gore, 75 years old, died Oct. 19 on New River of unknown illness, wife of Joseph Gore. Daughter of James and
   Susan Swinney.

28--William E. Harless, 18 years old, died in July of typhoid
   fever at Peterstown, son of Anthony and Judy Harless.

29--L. H. Hansbarger, 3 years old, died July 8 at Rich Creek of
   flux, son of John H. and Eliza Hansbarger. Born in Allegheny Co., Va.

30--Elizabeth J. Hansbarger, 9 years old, died July 10 at Rich
   Creek of flux, daughter of John H. and Eliza Hansbarger.
   Born in Allegheny Co., Va.

31--John Hinton, 69 years, died March 24 on New River of an
   unknown illness, husband of Evas Hinton. Born in Eastern
   Virginia.

32--female child of James A. and Rebecca Hutchinson died May
   16 near Forest Hill.

33--Sally Hull, 60 years old, died of cancer June 10 on New
    River. Born in Giles County, was single and daughter of
    Henry Hull. Reported by Harrison Shumate.

34--Elizabeth Hull, 77 years old, died of typhoid fever, July
    25 near Peterstown, daughter of William and Francis Hull.
    Reported by John Wills.

35--Mathew T. Jameson, 82 years old, died July 27 near Peters-
    town of typhoid fever, consort of N. Jameson. Born in
    Pennsylvania was son of John and Nancy Jameson. Death
    reported by Sally Brown.

36--Nancy Jameson, 77 years old, died July 28 near Peterstown
    of typhoid fever, wife of Mathew Jameson. Born in Rock-
    bridge Co., Va., was daughter of James and Sarah Patton.
    Death reported by Sally Brown.

37--Charles B. Johnson, 3 days old, died of fever July 16 at
    Wolf Creek, son of Caleb E. Johnson.

38--Mary A. Johnson, 23 years, 7 months, died Feby. 23 of pn-
    eumonia at Wolf Creek, wife of Caleb E. Johnson. Parents
    were John and Mary Argabrite, born in Greenbrier County.

39--Lewis Keaton, 21 years, 1 month, died March 28 near Spring-
    field of fever, son of Thompson and Polly Keaton. Reported
    by William M. Mann.

40--Almyra Keatly, 30 years and 7 months, died of "pleurisy,"
    Dec. 27 at Stinking Lick, wife of Henry keatly. Born in
    Bedford Co., Va., daughter of Ro. and Mary Hart.

41--Nancy Lawrence died Dec. 10 at age 77 years in Raleigh Co.
    of consumption, wife of William Lawrence. Born in Eastern
    Virginia was daughter of Charles and Nancy Brocken.

42--Hutchinson E. Lawrence, 6 years, 5 months, died July 24 at
    Rich Creek of "tyfoid fever," son of James and M. Lawrence

43--Joseph Lively Sr., 85 years old, died Feb. 15 at Stoney
    Creek of "paulsey. Born in Albermarle Co., Va., son of
    Benjamin Lively. Reported by rardiman G. Lively.

44--Fielding Meadows, 58 years, 2 months, died near Peterstown
    June 27. Wife was Tempy. Born in Monroe County, son of
    F. and Franky Meadows.

45--John L. Meadows, 11 months, died Aug. 17 at Rich Creek
    of fever, son of James and Lucy Meadows.

46--Mary Mann, 37 years, 8 months, died Aug. 4 of typhoid fever,
    wife of Squire Mann. Daughter of James and Nancy Mann.
47--Calvin A. Mann, 11 years, 2 months, died of typhoid fever,
    Aug. 4 at Rich Creek, son of Squire and Mary Mann.

48--Julia Mann, 2 months old, died July 28 at Rich Creek of
   typhoid fever, daughter of Squire and Mary Mann.

49--Ananias J. A. Meador, 3 years old, died of croup Dec. 29,
   son of L. and Mary meador.

50--William E. Miller, 4 months old, died at Indian Creek of
   scrofula, son of Henry and Delila Miller.

51--Allen, slave of John Peters died at age 5 years of typhoid
   fever at Peterstown.

52--Elisha G. Peck, 48 years, died April 9 at Peterstown of
   typhoid fever, son of Jacob Peck. Wife was Margarett Peck.
   Reproted by George H. Peck.

53--Margarett Peck died at Peterstown of typhoid fever, wife
   of Elisha G. Peck and daughter of John and Cynthia Peters.

54--Loami Pack, 71 years, 3 months, died July 26 at Brush Creek
   of flux, wife of James Pack. Reported by Samuel C. Pack.
   Parents were Saml. and Mary Pack. Age changed from 17 years.

55--Susan C. Peters, 87 years, 11 months, died of old age Dec.
   12 on New River Hill, wife of John Peters Sr. Born in Pennsylvania daughter of Christana Longaker.

56--Malinda M. Peters, 16 years, 4 months, died July 5 at Peterstown of typhoid fever, daughter of John A. and Rebecca
   Peters.

57--Martha A. Rains, 21 years, 1 month, died Feby. 28 of
   consumption at Droping Lick, daughter of William and Mary
   Rains.

58--Clara A. Spangler, 15 years, 11 months, died May 20 at
   Peterstown of "tyfoid fever." Son of Charles and Rhoda
   Spangler.

59--Nancy, 26, slave of Charles Spangler, died April of typhoid
   fever near Peterstown.
60--Aggy, slave of Charles Spangler, died at age 60 years, of
   typoid fever, near Peterstown.
61--Jno A. Spangler, 1 years, 7 months, died of typhoid Dec. 30.
62--Benjamin T. Spangler, 2 years, 7 months, died Dec. 28 of croup.
63--Eliza A. Spangler, died March 1 at age 15 years, 7 months,
   3 days of typhoid fever.
64--George A. Spangler, 2 years 3 months, 6 days died Feb. 14 of
   typhoid fever at Peterstown.

65--Mary E. Spangler died April 19 near Peterstown of
    typhoid fever, wife of George Spangler. Born in Giles
    County, was daughter of Josiah and Sarah Hale.

66--Rosa L. Spangler, 1 year, 4 months, died near Peterstown
    Feb. 14 of typhoid fever, daughter of G. A. and M. E.
    Spangler. Born in Monroe County.

67--George A. Spangler, 3 days old, died in June at Peters-
    town of typhoid fever, son of G. A. and M. E. Spangler

68--John, 12 years old, slave of John A. Spangler, died of
    typhoid fever.

69--G. M. Spangler, 8 years, 2 months, 9 days, died Aug. 8
    at Valley of typhoid fever, son of Daniel and Sarah
    Spangler.

70--Sarah E. Spangler , 5 years old, died Aug. 25 at Valley
    of typhoid fever, daughter of Daniel and Sarah Spangler.

71--Rich'd D. Shanklin, 36 years, 3 months, 16 days, died
    Aug. 9 at Hands Creek of typhoid fever, reported by wife,
    Caroline Shanklin. Son of A. and Nancy Shanklin.

72--William A. Shanklin, 5 years, 8 months, 7 days, died July
    13 at Hands Creek of typhoid fever, son of R. D. and Car-
    oline Shanklin.

73--Elizabeth A. Shanklin, 9 months, died July 14 at Hands
    Creek of typhoid fever, daughter of R. D. and Caroline
    Shanklin.

74--George Stevenson, 77 years, died April 11 on New River of
    typhoid fever, husband of Mary Stevenson. Born in East-
    ern Virginia, son of Hannah Stevenson. Death reported
    by Arch'd Mann, relation.

75--Mary Stevenson, 68 years old, died Oct. 14 on New River
    of dropsy, wife of George Stevenson. Born in Monore Co.,
    was daughter of Jno and N. Canterbury. Death reported by
    Arch'd Mann, relation.

76--James W. Townsly, 6 months, 5 days, died Aug. 7 near Peter-
    stown of flux, son of Thomas and Nancy Townsly.

77--Mary L. Tiffany, 10 years, 7 months, 28 days, died July 19
    at Rich Creek of flux, daughter of Hugh and Sarah Tiffany.

78--Sarah J. Tiffany, 2 years, 4 months, 8 days, died July 21
    at Rich Creek of flux, daughter of Hugh and Sarah Tiffany.

79--Andy J. Tiffany, 5 years, 5 months, 2 days, died July 21
    at Rich Creek of flux, son of John and Julia Tiffany.

80--Thomas F. Tiffany, 12 years, 5 months, 22 days, died Aug. 24 at Rich Creek of flux, son of Jno and Julia Tiffany.

81--Felix Williams, 42 years, 11 months, 5 days, died Feb. 14 near Peterstown of "tyfoid" fever, son of "Felux" and Nancy Williams. Wife was Nancy Williams.

82--Fleming W. Warren, 4 months, 2 days, died Feb. 9 at Wolf Creek of measles, son of W. J. and Delila Warren.

83--Marlin V. Wheeler, 19 years, 9 mohths, 10 days, was murdered June 2 at Elk's Knob. Son of Robert and M. Wheeler. Wife was Sarah Wheeler.

84--Sarah Woodram, 43 years, 6 months, 19 days, died Dec. 4 near Wolf Creek of "tyfoid fever," wife of H. Woodram. Daughter of J. and A Milburn.

85--Amanda J. Crotchin, 78 years old, died March 4 near Peterstown of tyfoid fever, wife of Wolf Crotshin. Daughter of Thos. and Julia Hobbs.

86--P. S. Rice, 17 years, died March 4 near Peterstown of tyfoid fever, son of William and Ellen Rice. Death reported by Wolf Crotchin, friend.

87--Sarah A. Diamond, 41 years, 7 months, 29 days, died April 30 at Stoney Creek of consumption, daughter of William and Nancy Rutlege and wife of A. K. Diamond.

88--Charles Diamond, 1 months, 13 days, died July 25 at Stoney Creek, son of A. K. and S. A. Diamond.

1859

CYNTHIA PETERS

PETERSTOWN CEMETERY

1--Francis M. Croser, 16 years, 6 days, died Feb. 1 of typhoid fever, son of Andrew D. and Elizabeth Croser. Born in Monroe County.

2--Mary M. Jarvis, 2 months, 6 days, died in September, daughter of Field W. and Jane Jarvis.

3--Ellen, a slave, belonging to Mathew Campbell, died July 16 at age 16 years. Born in Monroe County.

4--William Brown, 52 years, 8 months, 10 days, died Dec. 29 of "intemperance." A carpenter and widower, was son of John and Mary Brown.

5--Sarah Boden, 52 years, died Sept. 13 of consumption. daughter of John and Catharine Boden. Born in Monroe County. Death reported by daughter, Catharine Boden.

6--Julison Burditt, 3 years, died Sept. 3 of scarlet fever, child of Jackson and Eliz. Burditt.

7--Andrew Miller, 86 years old, died April 22 of consumption, farmer and widower. Born in Scotland. Death reported by son Andrew Y. Miller.

8--Emma J. Boyd, 4 years, 6 months, died Aug. 17 of scarlet fever, daughter of Thomas and Margaret Miller.

9--William Howard, 55 years, 4 months, died Aug. 18 of rheumatism, son of Jacob Howard. Was married. Death reported by son, Isaac Howard.

10--Francis Dunsmore, 7 years, 5 months, 2 days, died Sept. 21 of scarlet fever, child of John A. and Francis Dunsmore.

11--Sarah E. McMann, 4 years, 9 months, 18 days, died Sept. 2 of scarlet fever, daughter of William and Isabella McMann.

12--10 days old female died March 25, child of Edward and Julia A. Carnifix.

13--Andrew J. Higginbothan, 3 years, 10 months, died Aug. 4 of flux, son of Andrew and Sarah A. Higginbothan.

14--Margaret L. Young died May 1 at age 20 years in childbirth. Born in Greenbrier County was wife of Christopher Young. Was daughter of Archibald Hall. Death reported by Robert Young, father-in-law.

15--10 day old female died March 16, child of M. and Mary Winebrinner.

16--Jane W. Fullin, 8 years, 5 months, 27 days, died July 15 of
flux, daughter of John and Cynthia Fullin.

17--Mary A. Crosier 27 years, 2 months, 10 days, died May 29 of
consumption, wife of Philip B. Crosier. Born in Monroe Co.,
daughter of Anderson and Agnes Brown.

18--Catharine Bradley, 65 years, 3 months, died July 20 of consumption. Death was reported by Silvester Bradley, son.
Daughter of John and Margaret Shires.

19--Mary M. Bland, 22 years, 2 months, 3 days, died Feb. 20 of
measles, wife of Thomas Bland. Was born in Giles County.

20--Mary J. Nelson, 25 years, 1 months, died April 7 of scarlet
fever, wife of William F. Nelson. Born in Monroe County, daughter of John W. and Sarah Francis.

21--William M. Nelson, 67 years, died Dec. 24 of disease of the
heart. A farmer, his death was reported by a son, William
F. Nelson.

22--Archd Handly, 84 years old, died Feb. 20 of "gravel." Wife
was Susan Handly. Death reported by Mary Walker, daughter.

23--Elizabeth A. Cart, 22 years, 2 months, died Feb. 3 of consumption, wife of John A. C. Cart. Born in Fayette County,
was daughter of John Meadows.

24--Ann Eliza Young, 5 months, died June 17, daughter of James
G. and Margaret Young.

25--Oliver Lee Burwell, 2 years, 8 months, died in December of
scarlet fever, son of Amanda Burwell. Reported by George
Burwell, grandfather.

26--Pembroke B. Glover, 1 years, 6 months, died Aug. 25 of scarlet fever, child of John H. and Louisa Glover.

27--Silva, a slave belonging to William Erskine died April 6
At age 100 years old.

28--Mary Beamer, 60 years old, died Oct. 7 of dropsy. Death was
reported by M. Beamer, brother. Was daughter of Philip and
Elizabeth Beamer.

29--female, 2 months, old died June 2, daughter of George W. and
Elizabeth Reaburn.

30--Emily Smith, 9 months, old, died June 22 of disease of the
heart. Daughter of George W. and Martha F. Smith.

31--Holmes male, 3 days old, died March 6, son of James A. and
Susanna Holmes.

32--Waite female, 12 years, 8 months, died Nov. 20 of scarlet
fever, daughter of Anderson M. and Susan Waite.

33--male slave belonging to Clemen J. Campbell died at age 2
days, March 9.

34--male slave, 1 month, 1 day, belonging to Clemen J. Campbell, died April 10.

35--Louisa Miller, 26 years old, died of measles, wife of James
M. Miller. Daughter of Joseph and Margaret Bland. Born in
Monroe County.

36--Peter, slave of Robert McNutt, died of old age at 105 years
old on May 18. Was born in Philadelphia.

37--Francis C. Teays, 10 years, 9 months, died March 12 of scarlet fever, son of John and Malinda Teas. Born in Monroe Co.

38--Rebecca Bowyer, 32 years, 2 months, died July 5 of childbirth, wife of Lewis C. Bowyer. Born in Ohio, was daughter
of Henry and Abigail Dewitt.

39--Mary Bowyer, 59 years, 6 months, died Nov. 29 of apoplexy,
wife of Jacob Bowyer. Daughter of John and Mary Reed.

40--Mary M. Wickline, 16 days, died Oct. 15, daughter of Andrew
J. and Martha E. Wickline.

41--Amanda J. Ragland, 27 years, died Feb. 18 of consumption,
wife of John D. D. Ragland. Daughter of Daniel and Eliza
wickline.

42--Sarah Ann Martin, 9 months old, died July 4. daughter of
William T. and Sarah J. Martin.

43--Margaret C. Sams, 22 years, 6 months, died Jan. 16 of consumption, daughter of John B. and Margaret Sams.

44--Sarah Jane Wylie, 22 years, 6 months, died March 17 of consumption, wife of Jos. G. Wylie. Daughter of William Connell.

45--Elizabeth Beckett, 36 years old, died July 9, was a widow.
Death reported by James H. Beckett, son.

46--Moses, 83 years old, slave of H. Alexander died July 24 of
cosumption.

47--Billy, slave of Frances Dunlap, died March 18 at age 1 year,
2 months.

48--Benjamin, 12 years old, slave of A. A. Chapman, died Aug. 10
of consumption.

49--female slave died Sept. 1 at age 13 years of flux. Master
    was A. A. Chapman.

50--8 month-old male slave of A. A. Chapman died Aug. 16 of
    flux.

51--Mary Osborn, 72 years, 8 months, 4 days, died March 19 of
    flux. Born in Augusta County, Va. was a widow. Death rep-
    orted by a son, Jacob Osborn. Was daughter of Peter and
    Catharine Lohr.

YEAR OF 1859   (CONTINUED)

1--Otty C. Alderson died at age 19 months, 5 days, "choked."
    Died July 11 at Alderson Ferry, child of George and Mary Al-
    derson.

2--Selina Black, 18 years, 6 months, 2 days, died Jan. 21 at
    Rich Creek of tyfoid fever. Was born in Alleghany City,
    Va., daughter of J. A. and Rachael Black.

3--J. A. Ballard, 11 months, 1 day, died April 27 at Bee Branch,
    son of Harrison and Hulda Ballard.

4--E. F. Ballenger, 28 days, died Oct. 30 at Stoney Creek of
    croup, child of Jno M. and Sarah Ballenger.

5--William Broyles, 24 years, 10 months, 29 days, died April
    30 of pneumonia at Valley. A farmer, his wife was Mary Bro-
    yles. Son of Solomon and Sarah Broyles.

6--H. L. Dunn, 23 years, 3 months, 18 days, died May 19 at Rich
    Creek of typhoid fever, son of James and Nancy Dunn. Death
    reported by father. Was a farmer.

7--Madison Dunn, 50 years, 4 months, 10 days, died April 18 at
    Brush Creek of typhoid fever. Wife was Cynthia Dunn. Son of
    Thomas and Sarah Dunn.

8--Daniel Dunn, 15 years, 6 months, 28 days, died Aug. 13 of
    inflamation of lungs at Brush Creek. Son of Madison and Cyn-
    thia Dunn.

9--Lucy A. Dunn, 9 months, 17 days, died July 28 at Brush Creek
    daughter of J. A. and Eliz. Dunn.

10--Jesse Dickison, 61 years, 3 months, 8 days, died Oct. 9 at
    Valley of consumption, son of Jno and Nancy Dickison. Report-
    ed by wife, Catharine Dickason. (spelled both ways)

11--Levi, slave of Jesse Dickason, died at age 25 years Sept. 6
    at Valley of consumption.

12--Death at Stoney Creek (no other information)

13--C. J. Diamond, 21 years, 2 months, 1 day, died March 20 at
    Griffiths Creek of consumption, son of A. K. and Sarah Dia-
    mond.

14--James W. Dempsey, 3 years, 11 months, 28 days, died Dec.
    21 at Stoney creek of fever, son of William H. and M. Demp-
    sey.

15--Rebecca Epling, 23 years old, died April 21 at Wolf Creek,
    wife of Henly Epling. Daughter of Eber and R. Dilley.

16--Sam L. Ellis, 4 months, 8 days, died Dec. 24 at Valley of
    croup, son of Alex and E. Ellis.

17--Abram Fleshman, 64 years, 7 months, 4 days, died March 8 on
    Greenbrier River of disease of the heart. Born in Madison
    Co., Va., son of M. and M. Fleshman. Wife was Rebecca Fle-
    shman.

18--Thompson Garten, 49 years, 6 months, 14 days, died March
    24 at Wolf Creek of dropsy. Born in Monroe County, wife was
    Rebecca Garten. Charles and Eliz Garten were parents.

19--Mary George, 20 years, 7 months, died June 29 at Wolf Creek
    of consumption, Was wife of Jno W. George. Born in Monroe
    County, was daughter of Griffith and C. S. Ellis.

20--Mary S. George, 1 year, 7 days, died Jan. 27 near Centre-
    ville of consumption. Daughter of J. W. and Mary George.
    Reported by grandfather, Griffith Ellis.

21--Martha Garvin, 97 years old, died Nov. 28 near Centreville
    of old age. Born in Rockingham County, husband was Samuel
    Garvin. Was daughter of John Benson. Death reported by a
    son, Saml. C. Garvin.

22--Elizabeth Hansbarger, 34 years, 8 months, 7 days, died Jan.
    2 at Rich Creek of typhoid fever. Born in Augusta Co., Va.,
    was daughter of Rennock and M. Hodge. Husband was Jno. H.
    Hansbarger.

23--Lewis, 45 years old, slave of James Harvey died September
    at Red Sulphur of dropsy.

24--James T. Hill, 50 years, 11 months, 28 days, died Nov. 21
    on Greenbrier River of consumption. Born in Amherst Co., Va.,
    was son of James and Eliz. Hill. Wife was Mary Hill.

25--Emeline B. Hines, 17 years, 11 months, drowned in Wolf Creek
    April 10, daughter of William and Barbry Hines.

26--Michael, 54 years old, slave of James W. Johnson, died at Crop Road of dropsy.

27--Mary J. Kellar, 18 years, 19 days, died Jan. 24 on Greenbrier River of consumption, daughter of David and Mary Kellar.

28--William B. Long, 23 years, 2 months, 26 days, died May 24 at Valley of consumption, son of Thomas J. and Emily Long.

29--Delila Miller, 39 years, 10 months, 2 days, died June 21 of fever, wife of Henry Miller. Born in Monroe County, was daughter of Thomas and Judy Biggs.

30--Allen W. Miller, 1 month, 14 days, died July 14 of scrofula, son of Henry and Delila Miller.

31--Lanty G. Meadows, 13 years, 3 months, died Feb. 24 at Rollinsburg of pneumonia, son of Richard and Nancy Meadows.

32--Jno. McDowell, 72 years, 3 months, 14 days, died June 14 at Bradshaw Run. Born in Ireland was son of John and Easter McDowell. Wife was E. M. McDowell.

33--Martha Newman, 18 years, 6 months, 11 days, died May 22 on Greenbrier River, daughter of Jonathan and C. Newman.

34--Cyntha Peters, 64 years, 1 months, 15 days, died Feb. 1 at Peterstown of fever, wife of Jno Peters. Born in Monroe Co., was daughter of Saml. and Margaret Clark.

35--Jackson Rains, 47 years, died Oct. 5 at Rich Creek of inflamation, husband of Eliz. Rains. A farmer, son of Rob. and Eliz. Rains. Born in Monroe County.

36--Julia Rhine, 41 years, 11 months, 22 days, died July 8 at Indian Creek, wife of Geo. Rhyne. Born in Bath County, Va., was daughter of F. and M. Kincaid.

37--Sarah E. Scott, 4 days, died July 16 at Hungarts Creek, daughter of James K. and S. Scott.

38--Enoch Shanklin, 13 years, 2 months, died May 25 of flux at Centreville, son of Jno. D. and Saraha Shanklin.

39--Susan, 31 years old, slave of Jno Tiffany died at Rich Creek.

40--Thornton F. Warren, 53 years, 5 months, 28 days, died May 9 near X Road, husband of Sarah Warren. Born in Harrisonburg Co., Va., was son of Uriah and E. Warren.

41--Jas. M. Williams, 2 months, 16 days, died May 18 at Brush Creek, son of Jno. and Celia Williams.

1860

JANE NELSON
WIFE OF
TRISTAM PATTON, SR.
APR. 15, 1786
MAR. 20, 1860
MOTHER OF FOURTEEN
CHILDREN

LEBANON CEMETERY

1--Rachael W. Brown, 3 years old, died Jan. 30 near Salt Sulphur
   of scarlet fever, daughter of Alex and Mary Brown. (Alexander Brown).

2--Rachael Boyd, 27 years, 13 days, died Jan. 2 at Bickett's
   Knob of consumption, daughter of Robert and Catherine Boyd.

3--William Boyd, 30 years old, died Jan. 24 at Rocky Point of
   "wound of gun." A tavern keeper, he was son of Nelly Boyd.
   Was married.

4--Elizabeth Beamer died Dec. 24 at Hillsdale of bilious fever,
   daughter of B. F. and E. C. Beamer.

5--Allen F. Bland. 2 years old, died Oct. 1 at W. T. Creek of
   flux, son of G. W. and M. W. Bland.

6--Margaret Bland, 50 years old, died in September at W. T. Creek
   daughter of George and Sarah Bland. Death reported by Thos.
   H. Bland.

7--William A. Bland, 17 years old, died Oct. 10 of consumption
   at W. T. Creek, son of Jos. and M. Bland. Reported by Thos H.
   Bland, brother.

8--Jacob Baker, 72 years old, died July 17 at Sweet Spring Valley
   of rheumatism, son of Adam and C. Baker. Death reported by
   Chapman J. Baker, son.

9--Charles A. Carr, 6 years old, died May 20 at Rocky Point of
   worms, son of Mary Carr. Reported by James Dunsmore, employer.

10--Isaac W. Campbell, 49 years, died April 17 at Pickaway of
    liver complaint, death reported by his widow. Son of Robert and
    L. Campbell.

11--Jim Tom, 60 years old, slave of Andrew Campbell died of typh-
    oid fever at Pickaway.

12--Hugh, 7 years old, slave of Andrew Campbell, died at Pickaway
    Sept. 29 of typhoid fever.

13--Milly, 75 years old, slave of Mathew Campbell died in Novem-
    ber at Turkey Creek of old age.

14--Tavner W. Clark, 1 year, 10 months, died Jan. 7 at Christy
    Place of scarlet fever, son of Saml. M. and M. Clark.

15--Isaac Campbell Sr., 74 years old, died Nov. 17 at Potts
    Creek of dropsy. Reported by M. Campbell, wife.

16--Geo. W. Croser, 13 months, died March 3 near Union of fever,
    son of William H. and Sarah Croser.

17--Jas. C. Clark, 3 months, old, died July 28 near Union, son of G. W. and M. C. Clark.

18--Elorna J. Crowder, 18 years old died March 6 at Potts Creek. Born in Craig County, Va., was daughter of William and Sarah Crowder.

19--William Croser, 19 years, 10 months, died April 5 at Potts Creek of pneumonia, son of Andrew D. and Eliz Croser.

20--Emerson L. Dunbar, 3 months old, died May 1 at Union son Jno. A. and Eliz Dunbar.

21--Patsey, 12 years old, slave of B. G. Dunlap, died May 1 near Salt Sulphur. Parents were Nelson and Sarah. Disease of the heart.

22--Isaac W. Foster, 65 years old, died near Salt Sulphur Springs, reported by Isaac F. Ballard, grandson. Son of George Foster.

23--Ellen Fury, 64 years old, died July 12 at Forest of "nervions." Reported by Robert Fury, husband. Daughter of Moses and Mary Bostic.

24--Alusla A. Groves, 4 years, 8 months, 7 days, died Dec. 27 at Boggs of diptheria, daughter of Peter B. and Ellen Groves.

25--Sarah Griffith, 16 years old, died July 9 at Cove Creek of consumption. Born in Allegheny Co., Va., daughter of Jefferson and Margaret Griffith.

26--Jas Hardeman, 30, died at Union in November of dropsy. Born in Ireland, was a laborer. Death reported by Thos F. Parks, employer.

27--Samuel Hansbarger, 3 years old, died of yellwo jaundice Aug. 30 at Mount Prospect, son of A. A. and Ann Hansbarger.

28--Ann Harris, 65, died at Union July 4. Born in England was daughter of William and Alice Deacon. Death reported by Mary E. Lynch, daughter.

29--Geo. A. Kershner, 4 years old, died Feby 18 of scarlet fever at Brickett Knob, child of William and Eliz. Kershner.

30--Clayten Lynch, 2 years old, died in May at Union of hives, son of Jas. L. and Mary E. Lynch.

31--Alex'n Leach, 52 years old, died Mar 27 at Sinks of "Eusiphiles." A blacksmith was son of Joshua and Hannah Leach. Was born in Monroe County. Reported by Abner W. Leach, son.

32--Male died May 20 at Sinks, child of William and Susan Lynch.
No other information available.

33--John F. Milton, no age listed, drowned at Nickells Mills June
25, son of Pleasant and M. C. Milton.

34--Sarah J. McMahon, 20 years, 6 months, 26 days, died in childbirth Dec. 3 near Salt Sulphur Springs, wife of A. J. McMahan.
Born in Monroe County was daughter of Catharine Collins.

35--Eliz. McCommac, 35, died Aug. 23 at Peters Mountain, wife of
Jon McCommac. Born in Craig Co., Va., was daughter of Jos.
and Mary Smith.

36--George Moss, 76 years old, died at Gap May 23, was "wounded."
Born in Pennsylvania was son of Jacob and Polly Moss. Widow,
Belmira Moss reported death.

37--Sarah McDaniel, 75 years old, died June 23 at Rehobath of
dropsy. Born in Culpeper Co., Va., was daughter of Mathias
and Mary McDaniel. Reported by William H. Green, friend.

REHOBATH CHURCH AND CEMETERY.

38--Andrew A. Miller, 16, died April "was wounded" son of James
and Sarah Miller. Born in Monroe County.

39--Robert, slave of Owen Neel, and son of Susan died at age 26
at Gap of pneumonia.

MONROE COUNTY DEATHS
YEAR OF 1860

40--Adelia A. Reaburn, 11 years, 12 days, died Oct. 12 at Sinks
of brain fever, son of Geo. W. and E. M. REaburn.

41--Mary A. Reynolds, 18 years old, died July 17 of consumption
at Sinks, daughter of Francis and M. Reynolds.

42--Male child of Henderson and J. C. Reed stillborn Jan. 29 at
Holsapples Mill

43--Charles, slave of Joseph Parker, died of dropsy March 21 at
Hilldale

44--Albart, slave of Lewis Spangler, died of hives March 21 at
Union.

45--Seward L. Smith, 3 months old, died Sept. 28 at Sweet Spring
Valley, son of Lewis F. and Mary F. Smith.

46--Edith Steele, 60 years old, died of palsey at Potts Creek in
June, wife of Samuel Steele. Born in Monroe County, daughter
of Jos. and E. Wiseman.

47--Electra A. Vass, 2 years, 10 months, died of sore throat at
Gap Oct. 27, daughter of Allen C. and J. Vass.

48--Jacob Wickline, 83 years, 9 months, died Sept. 30 at Gap of
"motrification." Born in Pennsylvania was son of Jacob and C.
Wickline. Reported by William Z. Wickline, son.

49--Mary Wickline, 8 months old, died of hives in October at Gap.
Daughter of John E. and M. Wickline.

50--Peter, 30 years old, slave of J. L. Woodville died Dec. 31
at Sweet Spring Valley. Born in Botetourt Co., Va.

MONROE COUNTY DEATHS
YEAR OF 1860

1--Ellen Baber died May 15 at Quaking Asp Run of not known illness, daughter of P. B. and Cardine Baber.

2--Susan A. Broyles, 1 year, 4 months, 22 days, died of flux in
Peterstown Aug. 31, daughter of William H. and C. Broyles.

3--Catharine Becket, 40 years old, died of apoplexy Dec. 7 at
Gray Sulphur, wife of William Beckett. Born at Gray Sulphur
Springs. (Had Gray Sulphur)

4--Ruth Barger, 69 years, 9 months, 20 days died June 15 at
Bradshaw Run, wife of Jacob Barger. Born in Tennessee, daughter of William and Mary Handley.

5--Elizabeth Ballenger, 28 days, died Oct. 28 at Gromers Branch
   daughter of Jno. and Sarah A. Ballenger.

6--Peter Buckland, 28 years, 3 months, 19 days, died June 22 at
   Rollinsburg, struck by lightning. Born at Big Creek, a farmer,
   son of Stephen and Malinda Buckland. Death reported by John
   Buckland, brother.

7--Sarah Brown, 1 year, 6 months, died Aug. 15 at Droping Lick
   of flux, daughter of Henry and Nancy Brown. Born at Back Creek.

8--Mary J. Broyles, 35 years old, died May 26 on Waters of Back
   Creek, wife of William Broyles. Born in Monroe County, daughter of Joshua and Mary Canterbury. Reported by William Canterbury, brother.

9--Female Butt, 6 years old, died Jan 28 at Centreville, daughter
   of Shannon and M. Butt.

10--Jas. J. Cowley, 17 days, died Aug. 16 at Chesnut Hill, son of
    Geo and Rhoda Cawley.

11--Jane Dempsey, 42 years old, died of dropsy Jan. 27 at Griffiths
    Creek of dropsy, wife of James Dempsey. Born in Greenbrier Co.,
    daughter of John and Mary Rookstool.

12--Mary A. Davis, 3 years old, died Oct. 7 at Big Stoney Creek of
    croup, daughter of James J. and Mary Davis.

13--Sarah Dooley, 1 year, 5 months, died Oct. 29 at Howard's Branch
    of fever, daughter of Whit W. and M. E. Dooley.

14--Isabel S. Ganoe, 1 month, 14 days, died July 10 at Big Wolf
    Creek of flux daughter of Isaac N. and Nancy Ganoe.

15--Sarah Garten, 46 years, 9 months, 15 days, died Oct. 29 at
    Big Wolf Creek of "erycipolus." Born in Monroe County, daughter
    of Rich'd and Rhoda Woodram. Wife of Jackson Garten. Death
    reported by H. Woodram, neighbor.

16--Mary Garten, 24 years, 2 months, 16 days, drowned in New River
    May 18, daughter of Goodall and Jane Garten. Death reported
    by Judith Garten, step-mother.

17--Noah Holladay, 31 years, died Oct. 19 at Lick Run of disease
    of liver. Born in Eastern, Va., son of Israel and Nancy Hola-
    day. Reported by Mary Holaday, widow.

18--female, 3 years old, died at Big Wolf Creek of flux, daughter
    of William and Mary A. Kerby.

19--William L. Lively, 13 years, 9 months, died June 6 at Brush
    Creek of pneumonia, son of Wilson and Eliza Lively. Born in
    Monroe Co.

20--Jacob Maggert, 64 years old, died March 28 at Indian Creek, was drowned. Son of Henry and Eliz Maggert.

21--Maria, slave, 35 years old, died at Big Stoney Creek Oct. 15 of diarrhea.

22--Malinda Meadows, 90 years old, died at Pawley's Creek Aug. 22 of old age. Born in Eastern, Va., was daughter of William and Mary Garten. Francis Meadows was husband. Reported by Mrs. Wyant, daughter.

23--Jas H. Maddy, 1 year, 2 months, died May 10 at Big Stoney Creek of spinal affection, son of Absolem and Eliz. Maddy.

24--female slave died June 20 at Centreville of measles, owned by Anderson McNeer.

25--Elizabeth Pugh, 36 years, 7 months, died April 6 at Rich Creek of penumonia, death reported by Geo. W. Pugh, husband. Daughter of William H. and Catharine Broyles.

26--Jno A. Peters, 42 years, 2 months, died on New River Nov. 11, son of John and Cynthia Peters. Wife was Rebecca Peters.

27--Saml. E. Phillips, 69 years, died May 25 on New River of pneumonia. Death reported by Rufus Pack. Wife is Sarah Phillips.

28--Buchanan Peck, 3 years, 10 months, died Feb. 10 at Centreville, son of P. P. and Ann E. Peck. Born at Centreville.

29--Mary S. Rice, 8 months, died Sept. 27 at Peterstown of flux. Born at Peterstown, daughter of Jno M. and Eliza Rice.

30--Martha Smith, 7 years, 9 months, 24 days, died May 16 at Back Creek of diptheria.
31--Ugenia C. Smith, 4 years, 2 months, 30 days, died June 3 at Back Creek of diptheria.
Children of Ralph and Mary J. Smith.

32--James W. Smith, 2 years old, died Aug. 5 at Indian Creek of flux, son of Alfred and Mary Smith.

33--Alex'r P. Taylor, 42 years, died Jan. 14 on Greenbrier River of liver disease. Wife was Malinda Taylor, who reported the death.

34--Erastus Terry, 1 month old died June 14 on Greenbrier River of whooping cough, son of James and Nancy Terry.

MONROE COUNTY DEATHS
YEAR OF 1860

35--Fleming Underwood, 12 years, 6 months, 20 days, died May
    13 on New River of pneumonia.
36--Edward Underwood, 10 years, 2 months, 14 days, died May
    16 on New River of pneumonia.
37--Mary Underwood, 33 years old, died May 14 on New River
    of pneumonia.
    All born in Franklin Co., Va.
    Fleming and Edward children of R. H. and Martha Underwood.
    Mary Underwood sister of R. H. Underwood.

38--Bartler, slave of J. H. Vawter, died June 20 at Hands Creek
    of typhoid fever.

39--Margaret Vance, 83 years, 11 months, 27 days, died July 19
    at Wolf Creek of palsey. Born in Maryland, death reported
    by John Vance, son.

40--Rebecca Workman, 27 years, died April 8 at Peterstown of
    fits. Born in Monroe County, daughter of John and Permelia
    Workman.

41--Anna Wicle, 19 years, 21 days, died May 30 at Back Creek of
    "diphtheria." Born in Ohio, daughter of George and Lucinda
    Wicle. Death reported by Henry Smith, grandfather.

42--John W. Wicle, 13 months, died May 20 at Swopes Knob, son
    of Alex'n and E. HJ Wicle.

43--Emily E. Wiseman, 1 month, 13 days, died Oct. 20 on Green-
    brier River, daughter of Rich'd and Mary Wiseman.

44--Jos V. Walker, 1 year, 1 month, 15 days, died May 9 at
    Wolf Creek of croup, son of Andrew and Rhoda Walker.

45-John A. Wood, 4 years, 9 months, 25 days, died June 20 at
    Wolf Creek, son of Saml. and Eliz Wood. Death reported
    by Andy Walker, neighbor.

46--Susan Young, 37 years, died April 8 In Valley of jaundice.
    Born in Monroe County, daughter of Robert and Elizabeth
    McClowney. Death reported by Mrs. Ramsey, a neighbor.

1862

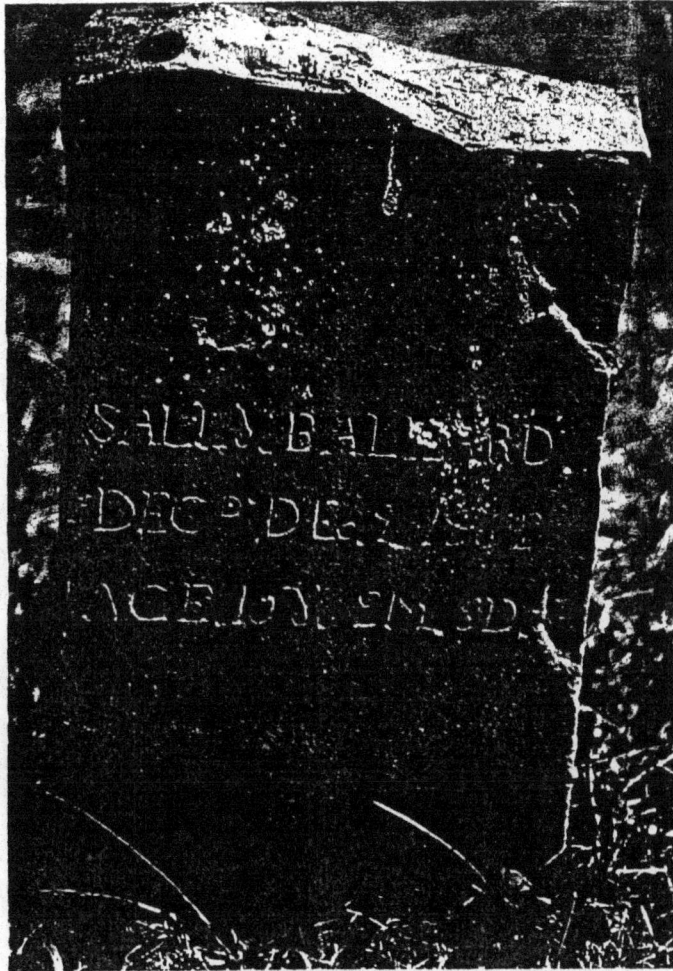

SALLY BALLARD
KEATON CEMETERY

MONROE COUNTY DEATHS
YEAR OF 1862

EDITOR'S NOTE: These records are not found in the Courthouse. On microfilm at Charleston in Archives.

1--Henry C. Alderson, 17 years, 7 months, 9 days, died Nov. 22 of diptheria, son of A. G. and M. Alderson.

2--Epha Adair, 1 year, 9 months, died Aug. 29, child of William and Sarah Adair.

3--Mary V. Barton, 5 years, 3 months, 17 days, died Feb. 23, daughter of Joel and Mary Barton.

4--Evan Brown, 12 years old, died Nov. 9 of pneumonia, son of G----and Ann Brown.

5--D. A. Bowyer, 7 months old, died Aug. 11, child of Silas and Sarah Bowyer.

6--Ellen J. Bobbitt, 15 years old, died in November, daughter of L. H. and Ellen Bobbitt.

7--Ballards Bare, 18 years old, died May 25, son of John and N. Bare.

8--George Ballard Jr., 80 years old, died of old age April 2. Ann was his wife.

9--John Bassham, 16 years old, died Oct. 11. Born in Franklin Co., Va., was son of W. and A. Bassham.

10--Susan J. Ballard, 1 year old, died Nov. 15 of diptheria, daughter of George and Della B. Ballard.

11--Allen A. Ballard, 5 years old, died (no date), son of Thompson and Ann Ballard.

12--Mary J. Collins, 7 years old, died Aug. 16, daughter of David and Elaine Collins.

13--Nancy A. Campbell, 51 years old, died Dec. 15 of rheumatism wife of Issac H. Campbell.

14--Joshua G. Canterbury, 34 months, died Jan. 25, child of Joshua and Priscilla Canterbury

15--Eliza J. Fleshman, 37 years old, died of fever in May. Born in Monroe Co., daughter of Jno and Sarah McDaniel.

16--Mary D. Foster died July 11 of measles.

17--William Finton, 72 years old died March 20, son of Richard and M. W. Finton.

18--Fanny Gartin, 22 years old, died of consumption, daughter
of Rich'd and S. Garten.

19--Benj. Green, 70 year old, died of gravel, son of Jesse and
S. Green.

20--William A. Gwinn, 2 years old, died of disease of brain, son
of A. L. and M. Gwinn.

21--Allen C. Hargo, 8 years old, died of fever, son of Octavia
Hargo.

22--Mary V. Harris, 8 years old, died of fever, daughter of
William and Sarah Harris. Born in Greenbrier County.

23--Isabella Haynes, 64 years old, died of typhoid fever, wife
of James M. Haynes and daughter of Alex and Jane Dunlap.

24--Isabella E. Jamison, 36 years old, wife of James E. Jamison,
daughter of Thomas and M. Dunbar.

25--Arabella F. Kilburn, 5 years old, died of typhoid fever,
daughter of Isaac and Mary Kilburn.
26--Alonzo M. Kilburn, 6 years old, died of typhoid fever, son
of Isaac and Mary Kilburn.

27--Mary Kissinger, 51 years old, died of cancer, wife of Jas.
H. Kessinger. Daughter of John and Eliz. Halstead.

28--Julia A. Kessinger died, daughter of Goodall and Almira
Kessinger.

29--John L. Kirby, 20 years old, died of consumption, son of
Rebecca Kirby.

30--Charles A. Kearnes, 4 years old, died of typhoid fever,
son of John and M. Kearnes.

31--Jas. G. Leftwich, 1 year, 11 months, 3 years, died of flux
son of David and Nancy Leftwich.

32--Louisa E. Lively, 11 months old, died of dysentary, daughter of R. G. and Martha Lively.

33--Allen C. Mann, 18 years old, died of flux, son of William
M. and Jane Mann.

34--Henry Miller, 86 years old, died of flux, son of Jacob and
Sarah Miller. Born in Rockbridge Co., Va.

35--Henry T. Miller, 7 years old, died of diptheria, son of
Henry and Delilah Miller.

36--Sarah J. Muncy, 37 years old, wife of John Muncy and daughter of Thos. and Eliz Biggs, born Giles Co., Va.

37--Nancy E. Nelson, 4 years old, died of croup, daughter of
    J. W. and Angeline Nelson. Born in Mercer County.

38--Elizabeth Phillips, 27 years old, died of apoplexy, wife
    of Nehemiah Dunn (Phillips) and daughter of Thos. and Eliza-
    beth Dunn.

39--Allen Pennington, 22 years, 9 months, son of Highland and
    Rebecca Pennington.

40--Cynthia E. Peters, 19 years old, died of consumption, dau-
    ghter of John and Rebecca Peters.

41--James, 29 years old, slabe of Rebecca Pack.

42--Elizabeth P. Pack, 58 years old, died of disease of liver,
    wife of William Pack and daughter of Robert and Mary Shanklin.

43--William B. Pack, 4 years old, died of diptheria, son of Saml
    C. and Amanda Pack.

44--Robert A. Pack, 2 years old, son fo Saml. C. and Amanda Pack.

45--Marinda Riffe, 20 years old, died of diptheria, daughter
    of Joel and Susan Riffe. Should be Clorinda

Clorinda C. Riffe

   Born Sept. 12, 1842

   Died Sept. 12, 1862

Buried at Dropping Lick

 in Monroe County

46--James A. Suttle, son of Will-
    iam B. and Eliz. Suttle.

47--Valentine Shultz, 72 years
    old, born Augusta Co., Va.,
    son of Valentine and Barbara
    Shultz.

48--Smith (male), 60 years old,
    son of John and Mary Smith.
(could not read some names, faded out)

49--Eliza V. Spangler died July 29, daughter of Chs. D. and
Agnes Spangler.

50--Allen M. Smith, 4 years old, died in December, son of
Saml. L. and Arabel Smith.

51--Amanda E. Skaggs, 22 years, died of typhoid fever, daughter of Jas. and Rebecca Skaggs.

52--Lewis Saunders, 9 years old, died of diptheria, son of
Robt. O. and Selma Saunders.
53--Rebecca J. Saunders, 8 years old, died in July.
54--Nancy A. Saunders, 5 years old, died Sept. 16, all children of Robt. O. and Selma Saunders.

55--Sarah H. Saunders, 4 years, 1 month, 19 days, died July
of fever, daughter of R. W. and Sarah Saunders.

56--Agnus T. Thomas, 19 years, died of typhoid fever May 11,
daughter of Rich. and Joana Thomas.

57--Jno. A. Taylor, 17 years old, died March 4 of consumption,
son of Jno. and Drusilla Taylor. Born Bedford Co., Va.

58--George Viars died of jaundice.

59--Isaac P. Vass, 19 years old, died of typhoid fever, son of
Jno. and Emily Vass.

60--Mary J. Vawter, 23 years, 6 months, 6 days, died of typhoid
fever, wife of Lewis Vawter and daughter of William and Sarah
Adair.

61--Zac F. Wikle, 6 years old, died of dyptheria, son of William and Nancy Wikle.

62--Fiel, 45 years old, slave of Polly Walker, died of typhoid
fever.

63--Permelia Workman died in December.

64--Dickson Walker, 16 years old, died Dec. 14, son of Andrew
and Rhoda Walker.

YEAR OF 1862

1--William W. Arthur, 22 years old, died April 20 in Richmond,
Va. of putrid sore throad, son of William and Mary J. Arthur.

2--Washington Arthur, 10 years old, died April 15 of putrid
sore throad, son of William and Mary J. Arthur.

3--Rachael Boyd, 29 years old, died of consumption, daughter
of Robert and C. Boyd.

4--Josephine Byrnside, 4 months old, died July 15, daughter
of Jno. and Eliza Byrnside.

5--Mary E. Boggess, 16 years old, died Oct. 10 of diptheria,
daughter of Samuel and Rebecca Boggess.

6--Allen, slave of Andrew Beirne died in July at age 18 years.

7--Alexander Bowyer, 23 years old, died Aug. 15 at Lewisburg
of gunshot.

8--Susan Ballard, 40 years old, died Oct. 21 of "mensturation,"
wife of Beverly Ballard. Born in Bedford Co., Va., daughter
of John and Susan Wills.

9--Jas. A. Bostick, 10 years old, died June 8 of camp fever, son
of Calvin and Charlotte Bostick.

10--Elizabeth W. Brown, 14 years old, died April 14 of diptheria, daughter of Alexander and Mary Brown.

11--Three-year-old child of Alexander and Mary Brown died May
16.

12--Female of Anthony and Lucinda Bell died Dec. 15.

13--Bragg female died Sept. 3 of typhoid fever.

14--Female of Jas M. and Mary A. Baker died June 1 of croup.

15--Carnifax male died March 8 of measles.

16--Jane Crosier, 29 years old, died April 8, daughter of A.
D. and Eliz. Crosier.

17--24 year old child of J. M. and Nancy Crosier died.

18--J. J. and L. J. Charlton's 6 year, 7 month old female
died Sept. 26 of diptheria.

19--Female of C. W. and M. Crosier died Nov. 20 of croup at
age 16 months.

20--Male, 11 years, 3 months of Jesse and Nancy Crawford
died Sept. 15.

21--Female died Jany 9, child of Daniel and Ellen Divine.

22--Male died April 15, parents, A. J. and Mary Daughterty.
23--Female child died of diptheria Nov. 22.

24--male, 30 years old, died of fever Nov. 2, son of Robt.
H. Dunbar.

25--Nancy Dunbar died Nov. 2 of fever.

26--Ann Dunlap, 15 years old, died Sept. 28, daughter of B. G.
    and Rebecca Dunlap.

27--David A. Evans, 4 years old, died of "soar" throat Nov. 1,
    son of Griffin and Sarah Evans.

28--James W. Faudrue, 1 year old, died June 14 of fever, son of
    Jas O. and Mary Faudrue.

29--Eliza C. Eggleston, 4 years, 8 months died Sept. 23 of
    "diptheria," daughter of Rich'd and Sarah Eggleston.

30--Lewis L. Griffith, 19 years old, died June 15 of fever, son
    of Jefferson and Margaret Friffith.

31--Margaret Griffith, 48 years old, died Nov. 28 of consumption,
    wife of Jefferson Griffith. Daughter of Edward and Eliz
    Bush.

32--Lorin D. Higginbotham, 25 years old, died Aug. 15, was "wound-
    ed" in Richmond, Va. Son of Henry Higginbotham.

33--Henry Harper, 40 years old, died April 13. Born in Green-
    brier County, was a blacksmith and died of pneumonia.

34--Margaret Hutchinson, 73 years old, died of dropsy of brain,
    Nov. 25, daughter of John and Rebecca Hutchinson.

35--William A. Hamilton, 21 years old, died Oct. 21 of fever,
    son of Saml. and Sarah Hamilton.

36--Samuel Hamilton, 59 years old, died Oct. 30 of "erysipha-
    las." Born in Rockbridge Co., Va.

37--Peter M. Jones, 3 years old, died Dec. 7 of croup, son of
    Mary H. Irvins.

38--Mary E. Jones, 3 months old, died Sept. 12 of disease of
    bowels, daughter of Charles and Mary Jones.

39--Margaret Jackson, 67 years old, died Aug. 1 of paralysis.

40--Susan A. Knapp, 2 years old, died Aug. 8.
41--Elizabeth W. Knapp, 7 years old, died Aug. 10.
42--James W. Knapp, 4 years old, died Aug. 13.
    All died of whooping cough, children of Albert and Mary
    Knapp.

43--John A. Leach, 25 years old, died May 23 at Lewisburg,
    killed in battle (Civil War), son of Robert and Susan
    Leach.

44--W. Lemons, 8 years old, died of diptheria. Parents were
    William F. and Martha Lemons.

45--Lettitia Long, 100 years old, died Jan. 28 of old age.

46--Mary J. Moss, 35 years old, died Dec. 25 of typhoid fever,
    daughter of David and Eliza Pugh. Born in Craig Co., Va.

47--Leah, 18 months, old, slave owned by H. W. Moss, died Nov.
    15. Mother was Mary.

48--Margaret McDowell, 78 years old, died Sept. 27 of dropsy.

49--J. W. McDowell, 35 years old, died in Kanawha City Sept.
    31 of camp fever.

50--Slave of Jane Miller, 55 years old, died of dropsy.

51--Child of Lewis J. and Nancy Mann.

52--Child of Jas G. and S. Miller.

53--Child of John and Matilda McCreery died of fever.

54--Barbara W. Nickell died of dropsy.

55--George M., son of Thos F. and M. A. Nickell died.

56--John W. Nelson, 42 years old, died Aug. 19, son of William
    and Margaret Nelson. Was a Deputy Sheriff.

57--Virginia Nelson, 23 years old, wife of William F. Nelson,
    died Sept. 15 of fever. Daughter of Samuel and Mary Bare.

58--Elizabeth Neel, 29 years old, died May 15 of diptheria.

59--Lewis, slave of William F. Neel died April 20. Was 51 years
    old.

60--Jacob A. Neal, 21 years, 1 month, 4 days, died Oct. 8 of
    camp fever, son of Walter and Catharine Neal.

61--Esbers Ann Powell died Nov. 15 of measles, daughter of John
    and Virginia Powell.

62--Charles P. Parker died May 19, was scalded, son of William
    H. and O. E. Parker.

63--James Parker died June 11 of fever.

64--Allen G. Piles, 26 years old, died July 26 of consumption,
    son of Jacob and Sarah Piles.

65--couldn't read.

66-John B. Patton, 23 years old, was killed by a bull Aug. 31, son of Tris. and Eliza Patton.

67--child of Jas. and Agnus R.------(cannot read)

68--Steven Ridgeway, son of John and Sarah Ridgeway, died.

69--Child of Thos. and Mildred Smith.

70--Child of John and Elizabeth Shepherd, Eliz, 31 years, died
71--Oct. 31 and Sarah C., 2 years, Oct. 23 of diptheria.

72--Lillian Sonaker (Slonaker), 4 years, 24 days, died Sept. 27, daughter of William J. and Arabel Sonaker.

73--Andrew E. Spangler, 4 years old, died Sept. 18.
74--Newton K. Spangler, 7 years old, died Oct. 14, children of Lewis and Elizabeth Spangler.

75--Amanda Shanklin, 3 years old, died, child of A. M. and Mary Shanklin.

76--John W. Shirey died of fever, son of Geo. and Margaret Shirey.

77--Elvira, slave of O. W. Summers.

78--John W. Taylor, 24 years old, was wounded May 31 at Lewisburg and died, son of Saml. C. and H. L. Taylor.

79--William M. Wickline, 21 years old, was wounded in Gallipolis, Ohio, and died, son of Jacob and Susannah Wickline. Died June 15.

80--Andrew J. Weiss died May 14, son of Abraham and Sarah Weiss.

81--Robert Wickline, 14 years old, died Nov. 12 of scrofula, son of John E. and Margaret Wickline.

82--Charles L. Wiseman, 21 years old, died Nov. 30 of fever, son of A. B. and A. Wiseman.

83--Sarah V. Waite, 3 months old, died Sept. 19 of disease of lungs, daughter of A. M. and S. M. Waite.

84--William G. Young died Oct. 28 of sore throat, son of Robert and Susan Young.

85--Oseola Young, 8 months old, died May 19, child of John C. and A. E. Young.

****

1865

JOHN E. ALEXANDER

GREEN HILL CEMETERY AT UNION

1--John E. Alexander, 58 years, 5 months, 11 days, died
March 17 of inflamtion of bowels, son of Mich' and Mary
Alexander. Widow, Jane Alexander.

2--male child of William M. and E. J. Bostick died Feby 28
of flux.

3--Virginia E. Bostick, 17 years, died March 24 of brain
fever, daughter of Jos. L. and E. Bostick.

4--John Brown, 88 years died July 20 of old age. Widow
was Polly Brown.

5--Robert Boyd Jr., 26 years old, died of "shot wound." Son
of Robert and Nancy Boyd.

6--Caroline C. Beamer, 9 months, 4 days, died July 4 of scarlet fever, daughter of B. F. and C. Beamer.

7--Alice Brown , 8 months, 9 days, died May 30 of consumption,
daughter of A. and M. Brown.

8--Mary Carlisle, 6 years old, died June 26 of consumption.
9--M. J. Carlisle, 9 years, 4 months, died Sept. 6 of flux.
10--George Carlisle, 4 years, 9 months, died Sept. 19 of flux.
11--Carolien Carlisle, 18 months, died Sept. 25 of flux.
All are children of Jas W. and Isabel Carlisle.

12--Martha F. Carlisle, 22 years, 4 months, died Sept. 15,
daughter of Samuel and Jane Carlisle. Death reported by
Jas. Carlisle, brother. Died of flux.
13--Amanda Carlisle, 18 years, died Sept. 29 of flux, daughter of Samuel and Jane Carlisle. Brother, James Carlisle, reported death.

14--Virginia L. Daughterty, 23 years, died May 29 of consumption, wife of A. J. Daugherty. Parents were William and
----Parker.

15--Mary Foster, 41 years old, died Dec. 20 near Union, wife
of George W. Foster. Parents were David and M. Tomlinson.

16--Mary S. Fry, 3 years, 9 months, died Sept. 9 of fever,
daughter of J. M. and Mary Fry.

17--Peter B. Groves, 11 years, 2 months, died Aug. 10 of flux.
18--Ellen Groves, 9 years, 4 months, died Aug. 10 of flux.
Children of P. B. and Mary Groves.

19--Mary Lee Hanley, 8 years old, died Oct. 22 of flux, daughter of Jas W. and C. Hanley.

20--10-month-old female daughter of C. F. and Virginia Hogshead died July 24 of fever.

21--George Kouns, 88 years, 4 months, died Aug. 12 of cancer.
   Reported by George Kouns Jr., son.

22--Grace C. Lynch, 2 years, 4 months, died July 30 of fever,
   daughter of J. L. and Ellen Lynch.

23--Laura Miller, 1 year, 2 months, 5 days, died Nov. 19 of
   fever, daughter of Thos. and Isabel Miller.

24--Mary I. Meredith, 21 years old, died March 1 of scarlet
   fever, daughter of Alex. and M. Brown. Husband was Jas
   E. Meredith.

25--Betty Neel, 12 years old, died Sept. 12 of scarlet fever,
   daughter of William and M. E. Neel.

26--Emma J. Nickell, 4 years, 4 months, died July 18 of fever,
   daughter of C. M. and M. J. Nickell.

27--Mary C. Nickell, 9 years, 1 month died of scarlet fever,
   daughter of S. W. and Ellen Nickell.

28--M. N. Nickell, 4 years, 5 months, died Aug. 15 of scarlet
   fever (female), daughter of S. W. and Ellen Nickell.

29--James F. Watts, 2 years, 4 months, died June 30 of fever,
   son of L. F. and V. P. Watts.

30--Elizabeth Broyles, 90 years old, died April 23 at Rich
   Creek of dropsy. Born in Orange Co., Va., wife of John
   Broyles. Death reported by Simeon Broyles, son.

31--Archibald Ballard, 24 years old died June 7 in Elmira,
   New York of small pox, son of Geroge and Delila Ballard.

32--Solomon Broyles, 92 years old, died March 2 at Lick Run
   of "dyspepsia." Born at Louisa Courthouse, Va., wife
   was Sarah Broyles. Death reported by Green Broyles, son.

33--7-day-old male son of Augustus and Rebecca Broyles died
   Oct. 29 at Lick Run of croop.

34--Lovel Broyles, 62 years old, died Oct. 29 near Peterstown of cancer. Wife was Elsie Broyles. Was a shoemaker, son of Solomon and Sarah Broyles. Death reported by William H. Broyles, son.

35--Thos. D. Crews, 55, died Oct. 19 at Dropping Lick of
   "compl disease." Born in Amherst Co., Va., was son of
   Arch. and Nancy Crews. Evealine Crews was consort.

36--Andrew J. Cummins, 19 years, died March 6 at Point Look
    Out of measles, son of Geroge W. and Sally Cummins. Born
    at Brier Run.

37--William A. Dunn, 29 years old died at Point Look Out of
    penumonia. Born in Giles Co., Va., son of Madison and
    Cynthia Dunn. Was single.

38--Elisha I. Foster, 4 years old, died May 23 in Monroe Co.
    of measles, son of D. N. and M. Foster.

39--Amanda F. Humphreys, 17 years, died at Indian Creek Dec.
    24, daughter of R. E. and E. J. Humphreys.

40--Mary Jane Martin died Feb. 26 on New River of "croop,"
    daughter of Thos. and S. J. Martin. Born at Sweet Springs

41--Harrison Pack, a free slave, 23 years old, died in Sept-
    ember in Ohio of consumption, son of Harden and Jenny Pack.
    Born at Brush Creek.

42--Andrew J. Peck, 39 years old, died Aug. 10 at Gray Sulphur
    of "dyspepsia," son of Bery and Rebecca Peck. Born at
    Hans, wife was Alafir Peck.

43--Elizabeth Pence, 85 years old, died March 13 at Indian Creek
    dau of Henry and Dresler Pence. Born in Rockingham Co., Va.,
    husband was Jacob Pence. Son, Henry Pine, reported death.

44--Christopher Skaggs, 28 years old, died March 13 at Fort
    Delaware of pneumonia. Born at Cross Roads, was single,
    son of Jas. and Rebecca Skaggs.

45--Vence (female) and free slave died in June at age 42 years
    of liver disease at Peterstown. Was servant for Wolf Crot-
    chin, former master.

46--Burns, 8 years old, whose mother was Vean, died of typhoid
    fever. Was a servant for Wold Crotchin, former master.

47--Arabel Jane Wickle, 3 months, old, died in July at Brush
    Creek, child of H. and E. Wickle.

48--Leroy Wood, 38 years old, died March 24 at Point Lookout
    of mealses, son of Robert and Francis Wood. Born in Alber-
    marle Co., Va., wife was Lydia Wood.

49--Virginia E. Wilson, 6 years old, died Aug. 16. Born at
    Sinks, was daughter of J. and M. E. Wilson.

50--Joseph Wilson, 50 years old, died at Indian Creek, son of
    Robert and Jane Wilson. Born in Botetourt Co., Va., son,
    J. H. Wilson, reported death.

51--Albert L. Allen, 1 year, 3 months, died Oct. 24 at Little
    Wolf Creek of "croup," son of Caleb C. and Mary F. Allen.

52--Malinda Brown, 21 years old, died in June at Dropping Lick
    of consumption, daughter of Anderson and A. Brown.

53--Jas. R. Broyles, 7 years old, died May 30 at Indian Creek
    of scarlet fever, son of George and E. M. Broyles.

54--John W. Canterbury, 17 years, 3 months, died Dec. 19 at
    Bradshaw Run of consumption, son of Z. and M. Canterbury.

55--James Ellis, 21 years old, died May 28 in Charlottesville
    of measles, son of Andrew and Mary Ellis.

56--Adelia Holdren, 3 months old died Oct. 15 at Bradshaw's Run
    daughter of Smithson and Nancy Holdren.

57--Asthan L. Hutchinson, 17 years old, died Dec. 10 at Forest
    Hill of fits. Parents were B. B. and A. Hutchinson.

58--Silas L. Hinton, 2 years old, died June 13 at Wolf Creek
    of diptheria, son of Peter and Eliz. Hinton.

59--James Y. Hill, 3 years old, died Oct. 20 on Greenbrier Riv-
    er, was burned to death, son of A. J. and P. J. Hill.

60--Ben Jackson, 80 years old, died June 7 on New River of drop-
    sy.

61--Wilson Keatly, 47 years old, died April 4 at Indian Creek
    of scarlet fever, son of Jas. and Lydia Keatly.

62--James W. Kerby, 9 months old died March 1 at Wolf Creek, son
    of Jas. and Lydia Keatly.

63--Wilson Lively 50 years old, died April 7 at Farmville, Va.
    Son of C. and----Lively.

64--Virginia E. Lively, 18 years old, died Sept. 22 at Swopes
    Knob of flux, daughter of Henry and E. Lively.

65--Jas. A. Meadows, 6 years 6 months, died March 7 in Fayette
    Co. of hives, son of A. and M. Meadows.

66--Geo. Rollyson, 12 years old died May 4 at Howard's Branch
    son of C. and E. Rollyson.

67--William B. Thomas, 19 years old died April 4 at Point Look-
    out, son of Jno. and S. Thomas.

68--Samuel Wood, 39 years old, died Feb. 14 at Little Wolf Creek
    of disease of the heart, son of Robert W. and F. Wood.

1866

ANNIE JOHNSON

AT WOLF CREEK

1--Jas Dunsmore, 8 years, 4 months, died March 2 of flux,
      son of Jas. A. and Jennete Dunsmore.

2--William H. Shanklin, 59 years, 11 months, died Oct.14
      of inflamation of bowels, son of R. and C. Shanklin.
      Widow was Sarah Shanklin.

3--Sarah Margaret Miller, 4 years, 9 months, died Dec. 20 of
      flux, daughter of A. G. and Susan Miller.

4--Richard Dickson, 74 years, 7 months, died Oct. 24 of spinal
      disease. Widow was Elizabeth Dickson.

5--Jane Young, 62 years, died Dec. 7 of palsey, wife of William
      Young Sr. Daughter of John and Polly Lynch. Reported by
      son, John C. Young.

6--George Burrell, 92 years old, died of old age Feb. 7. Wife
      was Mary Burrell. Reported by G. W. Burrell, son.

7--G. W. Early, 22 years old, died April 16 of "laudanum."
      Son of Jno G. and Hannah Patton.

8--Not named female, born dead June 20, parents, M. F. and Isa-
      bel Ralston.

9--Not named female, 8 months old, died Sept. 20 of flux, dau-
      ghter of John and Mary Hecht.

10--Margaret Boyd, 74 yers old, died Aug. 14 of fever, wife
      of Thos Boyd.

11--Thos. M. Nickell, 4 years old, died Oct. 15 of fever, son
      of Thos. F. and M..A. Nickell.

12--John A. Nickell, 6 years, 7 months, died Oct. 25 of fever,
      son of Thos F. and M. A. Nickell.

13--Not named male, 17 days old, died Nov. 7 of "croop," son
      of Jas G. and Mary Young.

14--Emily J. Reed, 6 months old, died July 24 of fever, daugh-
      ter of Henderson and Isabel Reed.

15--Not named male, 17 days old, died Aug. 28 of croup, son
      of Henderson and Isabel Reed.

16--William L. Bostick, 32 years old, died June 3 of consump-
      tion, son of David and Mary Bostick. Was married.

17--David I. Wickline, 9 years, 7 months, 12 days, died March
      14 of fever, son of D. and Harriet L. Wickline.

18--James M. Bland, 22 years, died March 6 of fits, son of G.
    W. and Polly Bland.

19--Mary V. McCommac, 17 years, 8 months, died Dec. 29 of fever,
    consort of Jonathan McCommac. G. W. Shives, father, report-
    ed the death.

20--Fred Randolph McCommac, 17 months old, died of croup, son
    of John and Mary V. McCommac.

21--Walter Neel, 52 years, died of consumption. A farmer, was
    married. Death reported by Jacob Neel, brother.

22--Margaret White, 22 years, died Dec. 7 of "coug" fever, dau-
    ghter of Sarah White. Death reported by Edward White, bro-
    ther.

23--Mary A. Parker, 7 months old, died Dec. 20 of flux, daugh-
    ter of James and Lucy Parker.

24--Lydia Lynch, 9 years, 7 months, died Aug. 21 of flux, dau-
    ghter of A. W. and A. J. Lynch.

25--Susa F. Anbler, 22 years, died June 4 of fever, daughter of
    Mary J. Anbler.
26--20-month-old not known child of Mary J. Anbler died June 5
    of croup.

27--James Burns, 15 years old, died Oct. 1 of fever, son of And-
    rew and Mary Burns.

28--John Roles, 14 years old, died Sept. 2 of flux, son of Ruth
    M. Roles.

29--Mary E. Scott, 8 years old, died Sept. 2 of flux, daughter
    of Hanson and Sarah Scott.
30--John Scott, 4 years, 1 months, died Sept. 4 of flux, son
    of Hanson and Sarah Scott.

****

1867

JOHN CAPERTON

AT UNION

YEAR OF 1867

1--Not named child born dead in March, parents were James and Margaret Walker.

2--Molly Patton, 23 years old, died Sept. 4 of fever. Born in Monroe County, daughter of Geroge and Mary Banon. Consort of W. T. Patton. Reported by T. Patton, father-in-law.

3--Mrs. Sophronia Hull, 76 years old, died Oct. 1 of "not known" illness. Born in Greenbrier County was consort of J. H. Hull. Death reported by son, J. A. J. Hull.

4--Not named 35 day old child died Oct. 1 of whooping cough child of C. G. and Isabel Shives.

5--Agnes Humphreys, 9 years old, died Sept. 1 of fever, daughte rof Jas. and J. Humphreys.

6--Sarah Parker, 32 years old, died March 19 of fever, wife of B. H. Parker.

7--Francina Archie, 49 years old, died April 7 of dropsy in chest. Wife of C. S. Archey. Mother was Polly Shirey.

8--Alice Park, 2 years old, died Aug. 14 of fever, daughter of Jas. A. and E. Park. (Pack?)

9--Sarah McCales, 76 years old, died Feby 7 of dropsy, wife of Thos. McCales.

10--Rosette Johnston, 7 years, 6 months, died Feby. 12 of disease of the bowels. Daughter of William O. and M. E. Johnston.

11--Margaret Carlisle, 45 years old, died Sept. 1 of fever, daughter of Jas. and Nancy Kelly. William Carlisle, husband, reported death.

12--Mary Miller, 84 years old, died of old age May 3, wife of Thos Miller. Death reported by Thos Miller, grandson.

13--4-month-old not named child died June 9 of fever, parents being D. and E. Taylor.

14--Not named 4 months old child died in Jany of fever, child of J. I. and M. A. Hayler.

15--Virginia Pence, 2 years old, died in May of disease of the bowels, daughter of J. H. and R. J. pence.

16--Henry Brown, 49 years old, died March 1 of consumption, husband of Dicey Brown, son of Jno. and Polly Brown.

17--Sidney Lowrey, 45 years old, died April 21 of not known
illness. Husband was G. W. Loury.

18--Frances Smith, 24 years, died Nov. 10 of consumption.
Husband was William Smith. Daughter of G. W. and Sidney
Laury.

19--Alexander Jackson, 68 years old, died Sept. 5 of not
known illness. Born in Indiana, Amanda Jackson was wife.
Death reported by J. W. Jackson, son.

20--not named child of S. W. and Eliza McKee died Oct. 1 of
fever.

21--Lucy Neighbors, 44 years, 2 months, 13 days, died in July
of consumption. Born in Rockbridge Co., Va., was wife of
James Neighbors, who reported death.

22--Susan C. Ballard, 3 years, 6 months, 5 days, died April
16 of whooping cough, daughter of Jno and Oliva Balalrd.

23--Caroline Ayres, 28 years old, died Nov. 25 of consumption,
daughter of Samuel and Susan Ayres.

24--Mary Alderson, 32 years old, died March 1 of consumption,
wife of George Alderson.

25--Amelia Chambers, 6 years, 3 months, died Jany 1 of whooping cough, daughter of Jas. and Paulina Chambers.

26--Rebecca Fleshman, 73 years, 22 days, died Feb. 5 of cancer, wife of Jon-a Fleshman. Born in Monroe County, daughter of Jonathan Roach.

27--Jane Huffman, 17 years, 3 months, died Jan. 23 of typhoid
fever, daughter of James and Mary Huffman.

28--Dunn male, 3 months old, died June 3, son of John and Jane
Dunn.

29--Geo Thompson, 29 years, 6 months, died Aug. 11 of cramp
colic, son of David and Mary Thompson.

30--Andrew Walker, 10 months old, died Feby 5, son of Chas.
and Mary Walker.

1868

JANE SPANGLER

AT PETERSTOWN

1--A. W. Atka, 63 years old, died May 11 of palsy. Born in Smith (Smyth) Co., Va., son of T. and Sarah Atka. Wife was Francis Atka.

2--Sarah A. Brown, 16, died in November of consumption. Unmarried was daughter of A. and Aggy Brown. Death reported by brother, A. C. Brown.

3--Simeon Broyles, 62 years old died April 12 of consumption, husband of Cynthia Broyles. Parents were John and E. Broyles.

4--Eliza Byrnsides, 52 years, 7 months died Oct. 3 of typhoid fever, wife of Jas M. Byrnsides. Daughter of John and Cynthia Peters.

5--Geo. B. Bragg, 6 months old, died April 10 in Mercer Co., of asthma, son of Thos and Martha Bragg. Born in Mercer County.

6--Mary J. Burdett, 30 years old, died Nov. 23, wife of Jas P. Burdett. Born in Giles Co., Va., daughter of C. and C. Callaway.

7--Martha S. Campbell, 19 years old, died May 28 of consumption. Unmarried, daughter of J. S. and E. Campbell.

8--William Donaldson, 68 years, died Feby. 15 of "dysentery," born in Greenbrier County and a widower. Moses Pence reported the death.

9--William C. Duncan, 15 years, 7 months, died Oct. 11 of inflamation of bowels, son of J. and M. J. Duncan. Born in Mercer County.

10--R. G. Dunn, 2 years old, died Feb. 17 of croup, son of J. A. and Eliza Dunn.

11--Male child, 20 months, of A. S. and M. A. Fleshman died May 30.

12--Male child of M. W. and A. L. Foster died Feby 28 at age three months.
13--Male child, age 10 months died March 7, parents being M. W. and A. L. Foster. (ages questioned)

14--A. M. Foster, 38 years old, died Sept. 21 of fever, wife of M. W. Foster. Born in Campbell Co., Va., was daughter of W. M. and E. Right.

15--Aaron Hargo , slave (free) 5 months old, died of croup in October, son of Malinda Hargo.

16--C. A. Huffman, 1 year, 16 days, died Aug. 30 of inflamation,
    daughter of F. and M. A. Huffman.

17--Male, 3 months, 21 days, died Oct. 30, child of William W.
    and L. C. Jones.

18--Lucinda Kepla, 62 years old, died Dec. 31. Born in Bedford
    Co., Va., daughter of John and Emma Craft. George W. Chal-
    ting, son-in-law, reported death.

19--Peter L. Lark, 5 years, 10 months, died May 29, son of
    Malinda Lark. Death reported by Nancy Lark, grandmother.

20--18-day-old daughter of James S. and M. C. Minner died in
    October.

21--Nancy A. Meadows, 46 years, wife of Rich'd Meadows, died
    April 6. Born in Greenbrier Co., was daughter of M. and
    E. Kincaid.

22--William G. Noble, 2 days old, son of A. J. and M. Noble,
    died July 9.

23--John Peters, 79 years, 10 months, died Jany. 11 of dropsy,
    son of C. and C. Peters. Wife was Eliza Peters. Death rep-
    orted by J. M. Byrnsides, son-in-law.

PETERSTOWN

CEMETERY

24--No name male, 7 months old, died March 24, child of
William and M. J. Ramsey. Death reported by grandmother,
Jane Ramsey.

25--Geo. Rhyne, 56 years, died Aug. 9 of cancer. Born in
Augusta Co., Va., a blacksmith. Wife, Mary Rhyne, reported the death.

26--Three-month-old daughter of J. M. and J. R. Stover died
in September.

27--Five-month-old son of H. V. and E. E. Shultz died Sept.
23.

28--Two-month-old son of D. and R. A. Shepherd died Oct. 30.

29--Jane Spangler, 70 years-old died Dec. 23. A widow, her
death was reported by C. M. Spangler, nephew.

30--William W. Tiffany. 27 years, died Nov. 23 of consumption, son of Jno. and Julia Tiffany. Born Tazewell Co., Va.

31--J. M. McD. Tiffany, 30 years old, died March 22 of consumption, son of Jno. and Julia Tiffany. Born Tazewell Co.,
Va.

32--Five month old son of C. Thompson died March 23

33--Francis Boden, 32 years old died in March of unknown illness, daughter of Joseph A. Boden.

34--John Beamer, 70 years old, died Feb. 3 of "cronic rhema-
tism." Born in Germany, son of G. and E. Beamer. Death
reported by Mary Vanstavern, daughter.

35--William Connell, 77 years old, died of unknown illness.
Born in Augusta Co., Va.

36--Virginia Clayburn, 35 years old, died in July of unknown
illness. Born in Monroe County.

37--Isabell Charlton, 16 years old, died of consumption Feby.
27 daughter of Thomas and L. Charlton.

38--Nermie Cavanaugh, 2 months old, died Oct. 21, son of John
Cavanaugh.

39--Ann E. Campbell, 34 years old, died April 2 of penumonia
daughter of R. and S. Campbell. Consort of John C. Young.

40--Emmeline Wikle, 32 years old, died in October of consumption. Death reported by Mrs. Shanklin, neighbor.

41--Isabel C. Vanstavern died Sept. 10 of fever. Parents were
    A.P. and L. Vanstavern.

42--Hannah Triplet, 24 years old, died May 1 of childbirth.
    Was married. Death reported by a neighbor.

43--Alonzo Smith, 16 years old died March 1 of brain fever,
    A. J. and W. Smith. Born Allegheny Co., Va.

44--Benjamin Reed, 72 years old, died of paralisis, husband
    of Susan Reed. Parents were B. and Peggy Reed.

45--A. N. Huffman, 2 days old, died in September, son of A.
    Huffman.

46--Jas L. Hoke, 6 months old died of pneumonia in April, child
    of C. C. Hoke.

47--George Campbell, 1 day old died in September of unknown
    illness.   It listed Jacob W. Hutchinson as father.
    (Questionable?)

ELISABETH KEATON AGE 71 YEARS

KEATON CEMETERY

1869

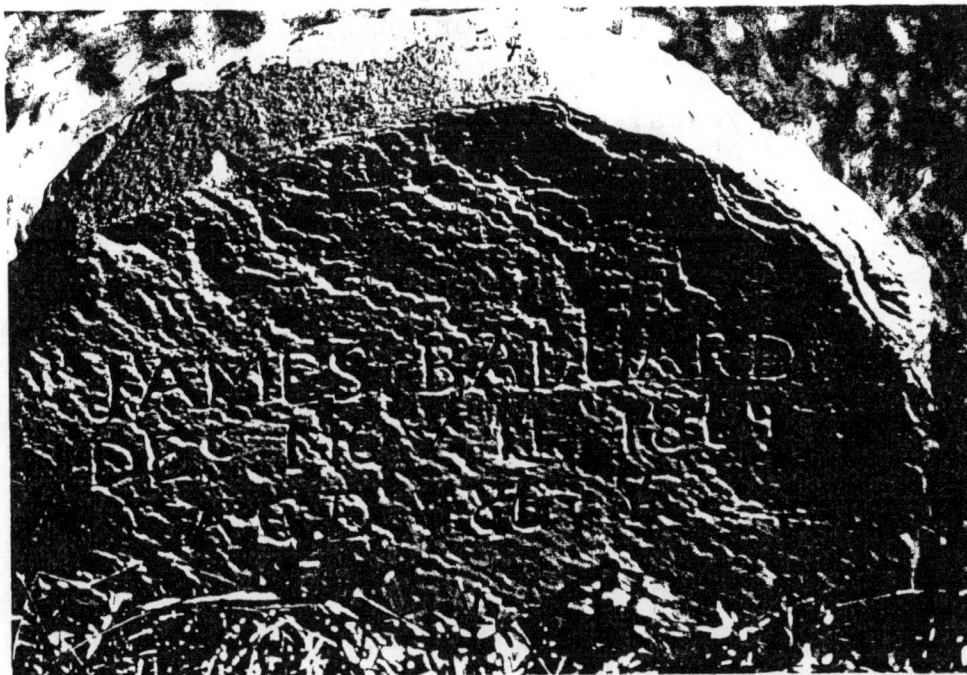

JAMES BALLARD   AGE 86 YEARS

KEATON CEMETERY

1--John Ayres, 78 years old, died in October of accident. Nancy Ayres was wife. Reported by N. M. Ayres, son.

2--Archibald Bostick, 75 years old, died of dropsy, husband of Sarah Bostick. Reported by grandson, Jno Bostick.

3--Louisa Broyles, 25 years old, died Aug. 18 of typhoid fever, daughter of Andrew and Sarah Broyles. Unmarried.

4--William Ballard, 94 years old, died in April of old age. Wife was Polly Ballard. Death reported by grandson, F. C. Ballard.

5--Lucinda Brown, 43 years old, died Nov. 30 of scrofula. Born in Franklin Co., Va., unmarried and daughter of Bird and Mary Brown. Death reported by brother, G.C. Wikle.

6--Elen Broyles, 13 years, died July 15 of inflamation of bowels, daughter of William and Nancy Broyles.

7--Two-month-old son of Samuel K. and S.J. Bonds died Oct. 4 of not known illness.

8--No name three-month-old son of N. A. and S. E. Dunbar died Dec. 16 of not known illness.

9--Sarah Ellison, 58 years old, died May 15 of cancer, wife of Frances Ellison, who reported the death. Born in Monroe County, daughter of Jno and Mary Beckner.

10--Susan Ferguson, 21 years old died of scrofula, daughter of Jno and Anna Furgerson. Was single.

11--Ruth J. Goodall, 25 years, 8 months, 17 days, died Sept. 24 of fever. Born in Greenbrier Co., daughter of T. F. and Delilah Warren. Husband was John Goodall, who reported the death.

12--Ida Gore, 3 months old, died of not known illness, daughter of Tucker and A. Gore.

13--Elizabeth Hines, 78 years old, died March 12 of heart disease, wife of Madison Hines. Born in Madison Co., Va., was daughter of James Jamason. Son, Jas W. Hines, reported the death.

14--William L. Jones, 3 years, 7 months, 3 days, died Oct. 11 in Alleghany Co., Va. of fever, son of A. and E. Jones. Was born in Alleghany Co., Va.

15--Henry Lively, 66 years old, died July 29 of epilepsy, son of Joseph and Frances Lively. Elizabeth Lively was wife.

16--Charles A. Mann, 1 year, 1 month, died Aug. 11 of inflamation of brain, son of G. and D. Mann.

17--no name child, 7 years, 3 days, died in July of not known
illness--parents, K. and Mary Mann.

18--Jacob Piles, 76 years old, died April 28 of not known illness. Born in Giles Co., Va. was son of Jacob Piles. A
farmer, Sarh Piles, wife, reported the death.

19--Mary E. Riffe, 1 month old died July 17 of inflamation of
stomach, daughter of S. and C. M. Riffe.

20--Jane E. Smith, 1 year, 9 months, died Nov. 30 of croup,
daughter of H. and L. Smith.

21--R. V. Shanklin, 20 years old, died Sept. 29 of heart disease, son of R. V. and Polly Shanklin. Was single.

22--C. A. Spangler, 44 years old, died May 14 of inflamation
of brain, wife of C. D. Spangler. Born in Monroe County
was daughter of James and Nancy Dunn.

23--James M. Spangler, 24 years old, died Oct. 12 of inflamation of brain. A blacksmith, was single, son of C. D.
and C. A. Spangler.

24--6 day old no name female died in March of croup, parents
being S. and Julia Smith.

25--Geo P. Suttle, 9 months, 17 days, died Dec. 31 of diptheria, son of William B. and M. Suttle.

26--Anna Smith, 79 years old, died March 19 of dropsy, wife
of Henry Smith. Born in Monroe County, was daughter of
-------Hopkins. Death reported by a son, William A. Smith.

27--Margaret Smithson, 92 years old, died Jany. 9 of old age,
wife of Thos. Smithson. Born in Monroe County, daughter
of Jno. and Mary Alderson. Death reported by a son, Geo.
Smithson.

28--Joseph McD. Tiffany, 29 years, 6 months, 9 days, died
March 23 of consumption, son of Jno. and Julia Tiffany.
Born in Tazewell Co., Va.

29--Simon P. Wills, 18 years old, died Dec. 25 of pneumonia,
son of A. Willis. Born in Giles County, Va. was single.
Death reported by an aunt, S. J. Willis.

30--Geo. Henry Bailey, 26 years old, died Dec. 1 of consumption, son of Andrew Bayley. Was a blacksmith and married.

31--Barbary Ann Burdett, 38 years old, died May. 9 of consumption, wife of Calvin Burdett. Born in Monroe County,
   daughter of Josiah and Sarah Curry.

32--Cary Burdette, 10 months old daughter of Bar. H. and Calvin Burdette, died of unknown illness May 9.

33--John Clark, 81 years old, died of unknown illness in
   March, a widower, son of Samuel Clark Sen. Born in Monroe
   County. Death reported by a son, Samuel M. Clark.

34--Jefferson Griffy, 61 years, 3 months, 11 days, died Nov.
   5 of dyspepsia.   Born in Monroe County, death reported
   by wife, Virginia Griffy.

35--Henry Harris, 10 years old, died Sept. 15 of consumption.
   Parents unknown. Under occupation it stated "neglected
   by a person."

36--Isa Walter, 11 days old, died in Feburary of unknown illness, daughter of Kinsobrin Walter. Father was a shoemaker.

37--Arrena Rutlege, 2 months, 13 days, died May 14 of unknown
   illness, daughter of William Rutlege.

38--Sarah Steele, 25 years old, died Aug. 25 of consumption,
   wife of Lewis Steele.

39--William Henry Steele, 6 months, 10 days, died Aug. 5 of
   unknown illness, son of Lewis and Sarah Steele.

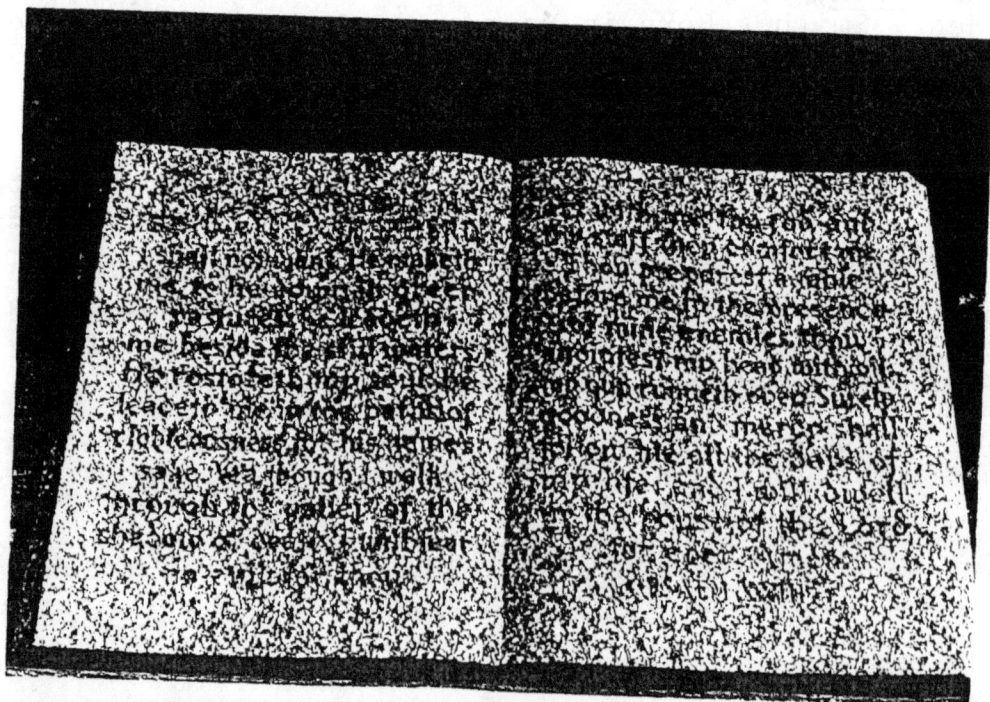

1870

ELIZABETH P.
WIFE OF
J. W. BARE
BORN
JUNE 6, 1825
DIED
APR. 14, 1870

1--Mary D. Brown, age not known, died of consumption in August at Salt Sulphur Springs, consort of Alex Brown.

2--Mary Bostick, 55 years old, died Aug. 3 at Hillsdale of nervous disease, reported by James Bostick, son.

3--George H. Bailey age not given, died July 26 at Hillsdale of consumption, reported by Andrew Bailey, father.

4--Emily C. Burke, 27 years old, died March 19 at Union of inflamtion of bowels. Born in Maryland, Rich'd Burke was consort.

5--Catharine Boyd, 71 years old, died June 17 at Rocky Point of consumption, wife of Robert Boyd. Information given by William Boyd, son.

6--Emese C. Baker, 7 months old, died Oct. 7 at Sweet Springs of inflamation of bowels. Reported by Geo. M. Baker, father.

7--Edwin M. Brown, 66 years old, died July 9 at Union of "deppepsia." Born in Lynchburg Co., Va., death reported by James McNeer, son-in-law.

8--Matthew Campbell, 64 years old, died July 23 at Salt Sulphur Springs of unknown illness. Death reported by John H. Pence, son-in-law.

9--Virginia Campbell, 56 years old, died Sept. 16 of typhoid fever. Born in Kanawha County, death reported by John H. Pence, son-in-law.

10--Harriet Crebbs died in Monroe County of unknown illness. Death reported by William B. Crebbs, father.

11--Isabella Curry, 15 months old, died March 18 at Second Creek of scrofala. Edward Curry, father, reported death.

12--Alexander Gray, 77 years old, died Aug. 7 at Sinks Grove of unknown illness. Death reported by Jno W. Gray.

13--Hugh Gray died Feby 18 at Second Creek
14--Amey Gray died April 7 at Second Creek
15--Allen Gray died in June at Second Creek
16--McClellard Gray died in June at Second Creek
17--Allen Gray died in June at Second Creek.
    Parents were Henry Gray, who reported the deaths.

18--John C. Higginbotham, 64 years old, died March 31 of consumption. Reported by Moses Higginbotham.

19--Clara Hull, 18 years old died Juen 8 of consumption, daughte rof Irvin B. Hull.

20--Hall female, 8 months old, died May 7 of unknown illness, daughter of William C. Hall.

21--Johnson female, 17 months old, died Sept. 21 of unknown illness, daughter of C. W. Johnson.

22--James B. Lynch, 74 years old, died Sept. 28 of palsey, reported by Jos R. Lynch son. Was son of James R. Lynch.

23--Geo. W. Massey, 8 days old, died of unknown illness in September. No other information.

24--Andrew McMahon, 37 years old, died Oct. 20 of unknown illness, reported by Jno Fullen, father-in-law.

25--John E. Mourning, 1 year, 3 months, died Dec. 15 of unknown illness.

26--Margaret Nettle, 75 years old, died of old age Dec. 7. Born in Monroe County was daughter of Calvin Bostick.

27--John W. Oyler, 2 years, 6 months, died July 2 of unknown illness, son of George W. Oyler.

28--Isabel Tygrett, 3 years old, died of unknown illness Aug. 6. Information said reported by Jackson Wickline, father.

29--Helene Wylie, 60 years old, died Sept. 4 at Cove Creek of penumonia, Was daughter of James Wylie.

30--Isaac Edgar Allen, 8 years, 5 months, died Oct. 23 of hives, son of Isaac and Mary Allen.

31--Margaret Allen, 25 years, 4 months, 10 days, died May 22, reported by Mary Allen, relative. Daughter of Samuel and Amanda Thompson.

32--Virginia B. Buckland, 31 years, 7 months, 29 days, died Dec. 15 of consumption, wife of J. H. Buckland. Daughter of Squiare and Ellen Wiley.

33--Ada Chambers, 5 months, 16 days, died April 20 of hives, daughter of R. A. and E. J. Chambers.

34--Mary Campbell, 46 years, 8 months, 20 days, died Feb. 26 of fever, wife of Andrew Campbell. Born in Giles Co., Va. was daughter of James and Mary Foster.

35--Correll male, 1 day old died Nov. 30, child of William and L. C. Correll.

36--Addison Dunlap, 60 years, 4 months, 16 days, died Dec. 2
of fever, reported by Chas. Dunlap, son. Born in Monroe
County, was son of John C. and Mary Dunlap.

37--Elswick, 10 days old, died July 17, child of Henry and
A. J. Elswick.

38--Lucinda Flint, 11 year, 6 months, 4 days, died Sept. 17
of flux, daughter of Bery and Mary Flint.

39--Annie Miller, 22 days, died Oct. 10 of hives, daughter
of John and Mary Miller.

40--John Miller, 63 years, 4 months, 2 days, died Oct. 19 of
"bilious fever," Born in Monroe County, son of Andrew
and Isabel Miller. Reproted by A. O. Miller, son.

41--Sarah McCulloch 64 years, 6 months, 15 days, died June 10
of flux. Reported by Mrs. Mustain, sister. Daughter of
J. and Betsey McColoch.

42--Samuel Pack, 6 months, 7 days, died Jany. 28 of cold, son
of J. and Elizabeth Pack.

43--James I. Pack, 5 years, 1 month, 6 days, died Dec. 26 of
croup, son of L. D. and Mary J. Pack.

44--Rosa Smith, 6 years, 9 months, 12 days, died Aug. 28 of
inflamation of brain, daughter of C. H. and Mary M. Smith.

45--James Wickline, 7 days old, died Sept. 24 of hives, son of
James and Mary Wickline.

46--Robert Young, 75 years, 4 months, 25 days, died June 24
of not known illnesss. Reported by G. P. Young, song.
Born in Monroe County, son of J. and S. Young.

VOLUME TWO TO FOLLOW WITH OBITS FROM MONROE WATCHMAN
PLUS RECORDS FROM THE COURTHOUSE FILES.

INDEX

Year of 1856
Andrew Bastin, Been slave
Jane M. Boyd
Nancy Jane Brown
Archibald-Butt slave
Louisa Bowyer

Year of 1857
Robert Bland
Jacob G. Baker
James E. Bostick
Virinda C. Been
Nathan Boyd
Edith Boggess
Allen M. Bassham
Lucy Broyles
Broyles child
Elizabeth Baber
Winslow Ballard
Jas. L. Bostick
Elizabeth Ballenger

Year of 1858
Catharine Boyd
William--Been slave
Adline Burns
William Buckland
Sarah Broyles
Lewis C. Ballard
Catharine Ballard

Year of 1859
William Brown
Sarah Boden
Julison Burditt
Emma J. Boyd
Catharine Bradley
Mary M. Bland
Oliver Lee Burwell
Mary Beamer
Rebecca Bowyer
Mary Bowyer
Elizabeth Beckett
Selinda Black
J. A. Ballard
E. F. Ballenger
William Broyles

Year of 1860
Rachael W. Brown
Rachael Boyd
William Boyd
Elizabeth Beamer
Allen F. Bland
Margaret Bland
William A. Bland

Year of 1860
Jacob Baker
Ellen Baber
Susan A. Broyles
Catharine Becket
Ruth Barger
Elizabeth Ballenger
Peter Buckland
Sarah Brown
Mary J. Broyles
female Butt

Year of 1862
Mary V. Barton
Evan Brown
D. A. Bowyer
Ellen J. Bobbitt
Ballard S. Bare
George Ballard Jr.
John Bassham
Susan J. Ballard
Rachael Boyd
Josephine Byrnside
Mary E. Boggess
Allen, Beirne slave
Alexander Bowyer
Susan Ballard
Jas A. Bostick
Elizabeth W. Brown
Brown child
Bell child
Bragg child
Baker child

Year of 1865
Bostick male
Virginia E. Bostick
John Brown
Robert Boyd Jr.
Caroline C. Beamer
Alice Brown
Elizabeth Broyles
Archibald Ballard
Solomon Broyles
Broyles male
Lovel Broyles
Malinda Brown
Jas R. Broyles

Year of 1866
George Burrell
Margaret Boyd
William L. Bostick
James M. Bland
James Burns

B's (continued)

Year of 1867
Henry Brown
Susan C. Ballard

Year of 1868
Sarah A. Brown
Simeon Broyles
Eliza Byrnsides
Geo B. Bragg
Mary J. Burdett
Francis Boden
John Beamer

Year of 1869
Archibald Bostick
Louisa Broyles
William Ballard
Lucinda Brown
Elen Broyles
Bonds son
Geo Henry Bailey
Barbary Ann Burdett
Cary Burdette
James Ballard

Year of 1870
Mary D. Brown
Mary Bostick
George H. Bailey
Catharine Boyd
Emese C. Baker
Edwin M. Brown
Virginia B. Buckland

C'S

Year of 1853
Mathew Cannaday
Lucy Counts
Mary Virginia Campbell
Martha Jane Campbell
Martha Jane Curry
Caperton slave
Ann V. Cummins
Milton Chambers
Mary A. Campbell
Mahala J. Canterbury
Elizabeth Campbell
Crawford child
Fielding J. Crawford
Siba F. Craft
Joshua Cart

C'S (continued)

Year of 1854
William H. Chatmn (Chathan)
John S. Campbell
Parthena Clower
Floyd Crawford
Mary F. Crews
Mary A. Chatman
Dicey Cummins
Eunice A. Coffman
Isaac Caruthers
Alice G. Crawford
Clark slave

Year of 1855
Oliva W. Counts
Anderson Carr
Agness Campbell
Jane Charlton
Nancy Charton
Nancy Cumbee
Mary Campbell
Margaret Christie
Campbell slave Mary Janie
John D. Clark
Campbell slave, Cornelius
Sarah E. Counts
Samuel Carlisle
William crosier
Campbell slave, Sarah Ann
William A. Chapman
Crawford male
Anky Canterbury

Year of 1856
Lewis C. Christie
William L. Christie
Mary, Campbell slave
Owen W. Chrisman
Campbell male

Year of 1857
Henley Chapman
Eliza Cummels
Jeremiah W. C. Crawford
Rebecca Clark
Samuel Clark
Elizabeth Clark
William A. Campbell
Rebecca Carden

Year of 1858
Polly Carpenter
Joseph Perry Chalton
Cook child

<u>Year of 1858 (continued)</u>
Carlisle female
Jno H. Cawley
Perliena Chambers
George Caldwell
Elizabeth Callaway
Nancy J. Craft
Amanda J. Crotchin

<u>Year of 1859</u>
Francis M. Croser
Ellen, Campbell slave
Carnifax female
Mary A. Crosier
Elizabeth A. Cart
Campbell slave
Chapman slave Benjamin
Chapman slave
Chapman slave

<u>Year of 1860</u>
Charles A. Carr
Isaac W. Campbell
Campbell slave, Jim Tom
Campbell slave, Hugh
Campbell slave, Milly
Taner W. Clark
Isaac Campbell Sr.
Geo W. Croser
Jas W. Clark
Elorna J. Crowder
William Croser
Jas J. Cowley

<u>Year of 1862</u>
Mary J. Collins
Nancy A. Campbell
Joshua G. Canterbury
Carnifax male
Jane Crosier
Crosier
Charlton female
Crosier female
Crawford male

<u>Year of 1865</u>
Mary Carlisle
M. J. Carlisle
George Carlisle
Caroline Carlisle
Martha F. Carlisle
Amanda Carlisle
Thos D. Crews
Andrew J. Cummins
Vence--Crotchin (free) slave
Burns--Crotchin (free) slave
(freed by Civil War)

<u>Year of 1865 (continued)</u>
John W. Canterbury

<u>Year of 1867</u>
Margaret Carlisle
Amelia Chambers

<u>Year of 1868</u>
Martha S. Campbell
.William Connell
Virginia Clayburn
Isabell Charlton
Nermie Cavanaugh
Ann E. Campbell
George Campbell

<u>Year of 1870</u>
Matthew Campbell
Virginia Campbell
Harriet Crebbs
Isabella Curry
Ada Chambers
Mary Campbell
Correll male

D'S
<u>Year of 1853</u>
Hendron Dickson
Dunlap slave, Banks
Alexander Dunlap
Virginia A. Dunlap
Dunlap slave, Jenny
Dempsey female
Conrad Deboy

<u>Year of 1854</u>
Dempsey female
Thomas Dunbar
George Dillion
David Diddle
Jane Deboie
Sarah Dick
Mary A. Dunsmore

<u>Year of 1855</u>
William L. Donally
Dickson slave Caroline
Julia H. Dunbar
Dunn female

<u>Year of 1856</u>
Joseph Dunsmore
Lewis Dunlap's slave
Oliver Fulton, Dunlap slave

Year of 1857
John Dickson
Mary H. Dickson
Mary Dickson slave
Susan Duncan
Lucy Dunlap slave

Year of 1858
Thomas H. Dunbar
Margaret Dunsmore
David W. Diddle
Eliza J. Dunn
Hugh Dillion
Jno Dunn Sr.
Delila Dunn
John F. Dunn
Henry A. Dillion
William N. Dillion
Christopher Dillion
Luther H. Dunn
Sarah A. Diamond
Charles Diamond

Year of 1859
Francis Dunsmore
Dunlap slave, Billy
H. L. Dunn
Madison Dunn
Daniel Dunn
Lucy A. Dunn
Jesse Dickison
Dickason slave, Leri
C. J. Diamond
James W. Dempsey

Year of 1860
Emerson L. Dunbar
Dunlap slave, Patsey
Jane Dempsey
Mary A. Davis
Sarah Dooley

Year of 1862
female Divine
Daugherty male
Dunbar male
Nancy Dunbar
Ann Dunlap

Year of 1865
Virginia L. Daugherty
William A. Dunn

Year of 1866
Jas Dunsmore
Richard Dickson

Year of 1867
Dunn male

Year of 1868
William Donaldson
William C. Duncan
R. G. Dunn

Year of 1869
Dunbar son

Year of 1870
Addison Dunlap

E'S

Year of 1853
Elizabeth Early
William Early
William Wallace Early
Eggleston female
George Evans
Elizabeth Ellison
Joseph Ellison
Jane Ellison

Year of 1854
Delila Eads
Polly Erskine
John H. Ewing
William Erskine

Year of 1855
Elisha Ewins
Alex'r J. Erskine
Mary A. Eddy

Year of 1856
James Erskine
Isaac C. Erskine
Kelton Eads
James William Ellison
Jacob Ellis

Year of 1857
Augustus Erskine
Charles A. Erskine

Year of 1858
James Lewis Early

Year of 1859
William Erskine
Rebecca Epling

E'S (continued)

Year of 1859 (continued)
Sam L. Ellis

Year of 1862
David A. Evans
Eliza C. Eggleston

Year of 1865
James Ellis

Year of 1866
G. W. Early

Year of 1869
Sarah Ellison

Year of 1870
Elswick child

F'S

Year of 1853
Barbara Ann Fury
Isabella Francis
Elizabeth Francis
William S. Foard
Andrew Fleshman
Margaret Fry
Mary E. Foster

Year of 1854
Jane E. Faundree
James Foster
Mary J. Foster
Susan Foster
Martha W. Foster
Thos H. Francis

Year of 1855
Eliz'th Foard
Martha Jane Falks

Year of 1856
John Francis
Isabel Francis
William Fleshman
William Henderson Foster
Thomas Jefferson Fry
William Alexander Fry

Year of 1857
Alexander E. Fullen
Jas. M. Fry
Ann E. Fry

F'S (continued)

Year of 1858
Joseph Fisher
Ellen Marthy Foster
Mahala J. Furgerson
Wiley Furgerson
Dr. Thomas Fowler

Year of 1859
Jane W. Fullin
Abram Fleshman

Year of 1860
Isaac W. Foster
Ellen Fury

Year of 1862
Eliza J. Fleshman
Mary D. Foster
William Finton
Romeluis Ford
Jas W. Faudrue

Year of 1865
Mary Foster
Mary S. Fry
Elisha I. Foster

Year of 1867
Rebecca Fleshman

Year of 1868
Fleshman male
Foster male
Foster male
A. M. Foster

Year of 1869
Susan Ferguson

Year of 1870
Lucinda Flint

G'S

Year of 1853
Lucy Goodall
Virginia Goodall
John C. Green
Garten female
Eliza G. Gibson

Year of 1854
Mary E. Gibson
Lucy C. Gray
J. S. Gwinn

Year of 1854 (continued)
Mary J. Gibson
Mary E. Gibson
Jane Graham
Mary N. Goodall
Mary E. Gilmer

Year of 1855
Jane Gilchris
Isabella E. Griffith

Year of 1856
Clementine V. Gibson

Year of 1857
Thompson R. Goodall
Mary A. Goodall
Joseph Graham

Year of 1858
Betsy, Gray slave
Gray slave
Samuel C. Gwinn
Joseph L. Gwinn
Rachel Gore

Year of 1859
Pembroke B. Glover
Thompson Garten
Mary George
Mary S. George
Martha Garvin

Year of 1860
Alusla A. Groves
Sarah Griffith
Isabel S. Ganoe
Sarah Garten
Mary Garten

Year of 1862
Fanny Gartin
Benj. Green
William A. Gwinn
Lewis L. Griffith
Margaret Griffith

Year of 1865
Peter B. Groves
Ellen Groves

Year of 1869
Ruth J. goodall
Ida Gore
Jefferson Griffy

Year of 1870
Alexander Gray
Hugh Gray
Amey Gray
Allen Gray
McClellard Gray

H'S

Year of 1853
Nancy N. Hawkins
Elizabeth Jane Hawkins
Lucinda Hutchison
Newton A. Hill
Barbara Hines
Harry, Haynes slave
Henry, Haynes slave

Year of 1854
Preston Hargo
Sarah E. Hecht
Sarah Humphreys
George W. Hutchison
Laura A. Hall
William Herron
Mary M. Humphreys
Samuel C. Humphreys
Lucinda Hutchison
Geo W. Harvey
Jas. R. Harvey
Hill slave, Rhoda
Edward D. Hill
John Humphreys
George Holsapple
James Hogshead
Harris female
Nancy Hutchinson

Year of 1855
ANna W. Hawkins
Sarah R. Handley
Alcestra A. Hanger
Richard Howard
Barbra J. R. Hoke
John Hutchinson
Cornelius Jasper Harless
John Houchens
John E. Humphreys

Year of 1856
Lucy Humphreys
Sarah C. Howell
Mary, Holsapple slave
James A. Higginbotham

Year of 1856
David Hutcheson
Joseph Haynes
Mary Herron
Sarah Ann Hinton
Rachel Helms

Year of 1857
Sarah F. Hutchinson
Hill child
Jane Hogshead
John Hogshead
Elizabeth Holms
John Hull
Martha Huffman
Humphreys child
Martha Hutchison
Joel R. Holden
Dorothy Harvey
Mary R. Humphreys
Manerva Humphreys
Mary A. Haynes
Jno J. Huffman
Alex'r D. Haynes

Year of 1858
Homes child
William E. Harless
L. H. Hansbarger
Elizabeth J. Hansbarger
John Hinton
Hutchinson female
Sally Hull
Elizabeth Hull

Year of 1859
William Howard
Andrew H. Higginbotham
Arch'd Handly
Holmes male
Elizabeth Hansbarger
Harvey slave, Lewis
James T. Hill
Emeline B. Hines

Year of 1860
Jas Hardeman
Samuel Hansbarger
Ann Harris
Noah Holladay

Year of 1862
Allen C. Hargo
Mary V. Harris
Isabella Haynes
Lorin D. Higginbotham

Year of 1862
Henry Harper
Margaret Hutchinson
William A. Hamilton
Saml. Hamilton

Year of 1865
Mary Lee Hanley
Hogshead female
AManda F. Humphreys
Adelia Holdren
Asthan L. Hutchinson
Silas L. Hinton
James Y. Hill

Year of 1866
Hecht female

Year of 1867
Mrs. Sophronia Hull
Agnes Humphreys

Year of 1867
Hayler child
Jane Huffman

Year of 1868
Aaron Hargo (free)
C. A. Huffman
A. N. Huffman
Jas L. Hoke

Year of 1869
Elizabeth Hines
Henry Harris

Year of 1870
John C. Higginbotham
Clara Hull
Hall female

J'S

Year of 1853
Catharine Johnson
Lewis Johnson

Year of 1854
Richard Johnson
Harriet W. Johnson
Clarenda E. Jones
Jones slave, Mary
Henry Jones
Simeon Jennings
Johnson slave, John

J'S (continued)

Year of 1856
Francis Jones

Year of 1857
Jas A. Jeffreys
Elizabeth Johnson

Year of 1858
Mathew T. Jameson
Nancy Jameson
Charles B. Johnson
Mary A. Johnson

Year of 1859
Mary M. Jarvis
Johnson slave, Michael

Year of 1862
Peter M. Jones
Mary E. Jones
Margaret Jackson

Year of 1865
Ben Jackson

Year of 1867
Rosette Johnston
Alexander Jackson

Year of 1868
Jones male

Year of 1869
William L. Jones

Year of 1870
Johnson female

K'S

Year of 1853
Sydney King
Elizabeth Kilburn
Jane A. Kearns

Year of 1854
Lucy Knode
Catharine Kouns

Year of 1855
Delilah Keatly

Year of 1857
Agness Kerby

K'S

Year of 1858
Lewis Keaton
Almyra Keatly

Year of 1859
Mary J. Kellar

Year of 1860
Geo A. Kershner
Kerby female

Year of 1862
Arabella F. Kilburn
Alonzo M. Kilburn
Mary Kissinger
Julia A. Kessinger
John L. Kisby
Charles A. Kearns
Susan A. Knabb
Elizabeth W. Knapp
James W. Knapp

Year of 1865
George Kouns
Wilson Keatly
James W. Kerby

Year of 1868
Lucinda Kepla
Elisabeth Keaton

L'S
William, Lanius slave

Year of 1854
Chs. W. Lively
John A. Lowe
Chs L. Lowe
Rupard N. Lively
Sidney M. Lively
Julia Long
Hugh L. Lynch
Hannah Leach
George Lowe

Year of 1855
Eliza Legg
Lewis slave, Oscar
Lewis slave, Ellen
Lewis slave, Edmund
Lewis slave, Sarah Ann
Simeon Jennings

L'S (continued)

Year of 1856
William W. Landers
Mary Lemons
Elizabeth Lowe

Year of 1858
Nancy Landers
Joshua Leach
Mary Ann Long
Nancy Lawrence
Hutchinson E. Lawrence
Joseph Lively Sr.

Year of 1859
William B. Long

Year of 1860
Clayten Lynch
Alex'n Leach
Lynch male
William L. Lively

Year of 1862
Jas G. Leftwich
Louisa E. Lively
JohnA. Leach
W. Lemons
Lettitia Long

Year of 1865
Grace C. Lynch
Wilson Lively
Virginia E. Lively

Year of 1866
Lydia Lynch

Year of 1867
Sidney Lowrey

Year of 1868
Peter L. Lark

Year of 1869
Henry Lively

Year of 1870
James B. Lynch

M'S

Year of 1853
Mahon male
Andrew L. R. Moss
Isabella Mitter
McDaniel slave, Charles
McDaniel slave, female
James William McDowell
Moss slave, Minda
Mann child
John Mann Jr.
Richard McNeer
McNeer slave, John Henry
Elizabeth Meadows
Maddy slave, William Pembroke
Nancy R. Maddy
Sarah S. Mann
Moses Mann
Mann male
Rebecca J. Miller
Francis Meadows
Caroline R. Mann

Year of 1854
Alex' C. Mann
Eliz E. Maddy
Michael G. Miller
Martha A. Mays
Nancy C. Meadows
Amanda Meadows
Polly Martin
Allen G. Mann
Rhoda Miller
Mary E. Mann
Nancy W. Mann
Albert Mann
Ward C.Mann
Christopher Mann
Rhoda Mann
Elizabeth Mead
William H. Mann
Elizabeth McGlamery
Belmira J. Moss
Edmund Meeks
Moss slave, Miller

Year of 1855
Massey son
Jonathan Miller
Mentz son
John Miller
Aaron Morgan
Mary A. Morgan
Miller male
Mary E. McNeigh
Mitchell child

Year of 1855
Sarah C. McGuire
Margaret Masters
Merit Magann
Maddy slave, Delilah
Sarah C. Meadows
Peter McGee
John A. Miller
Sarah M. Meads
James Mann
James McNeer
Stuart McCorkle
Andrew H. McNeer

Year of 1856
Peter Miller
Eliza McClowney
Calvin Moss
Martha J. Mentz
Lucinda E. McCommack
James H. McCartney
Archibald Swinney McGee
Samuel McCorkle
Meadows child

Year of 1857
Robert Mentz
Jennetta Morris
Nancy A. Morris
Elizabeth Mitchell
William L. Mitchell
Margaret G. Mitchell
Mary E. Mitchell
John Mann
Martha Mann
Ananias Meadows
Polly E. Miller

Year of 1858
Moss lsave
Lyddy Moss
Thomas McCaleb
Fielding Meadows
John L. Meadows
Mary Mann
Calvin A. Mann
Julia Mann
Ananias J. A. Meador
William E. Miller

Year of 1859
Andrew Miller
Sarah E. McMann
Louisa Miller
Peter, McNutt slave
Sarah Ann Martin

Year of 1859
Delila Miller
Allen W. Miller
Lanty G. Meadows
Jno McDowell

Year of 1860
John F. Milton
Sarah J. McMahon
Eliz McCommac
George Moss
Sarah McDaniel
Andrew A. Miller
Jacob Maggert
Malinda Meadows
Jas H. Maddy
McNeer slave

Year of 1862
Allen C. Mann
Henry T. Miller
Sarah J. Muncy
Mary J. Moss
Leah, Moss slave
Margaret McDowell
J. W. McDowell
Miller slave
Mann child
Miller child
McCreery child

Year of 1865
Laura Miller
Mary I. Meredith
Mary Jane Martin
Jas A. Meadows

Year of 1866
Sarah Margaret Miller
Mary V. McCommac
Fred Randolph McCommac

Year of 1867
Sarah McCales
Mary Miller
MCKee child

Year of 1868
Minner daughter
Nancy A. Meadows

Year of 1869
Charles A. Mann
Mann child

M'S (continued)

Year of 1870
Geo W. Massey
Andrew McMahon
John E. Mourning
Annie Miller
John Miller
Sarah McCulloch

N'S

Year of 1853
Peggy Nickell   slave
Mary Susan Nickell slave
Stephen Noble

Year of 1854
David C. Nickell
Neel son

Year of 1855
Nelson daughter

Year of 1856
Nickell male
John Neel
Ruth McNutt
Emma Neel

Year of 1857
Malinda Nettle
William Nettle
Brown L. Nettle

Year of 1858
Polly Neel

Year of 1859
Mary J. Nelson
William M. Nelson
Martha Newman

Year of 1860
Neel slave, Robert

Year of 1862
Nancy E. Nelson
George M. Nickell
John W. Nelson
Virginia Nelson
Elizabeth Neel
Lewis, Neel slave
Jacob A. Neal

N'S (continued)

Year of 1865
Betty Neel
Emma J. Nickell
Mary C. Nickell
M. N. Nickell

Year of 1866
Thos M. Nickell
John A. Nickell
Walter Neel

Year of 1867
Lucy Neighbors

Year of 1868
William G. Noble

Year of 1870
Margaret Nettle

O'S

Year of 1855
Elizabeth Owens

Year of 1859
Mary Osborn

Year of 1870
John W. Oyler

P'S

Year of 1853
Catharine Preston
Elizabeth Prentice
Julia Patton slave
Emma, Patton slave
Emanuel M. Pence
Milam Pennington
Harrison Pennington
Nancy Powley
William A. Powley

Year of 1854
Amanda Page
Elizbeth Payne
Martha J. Patten

Year of 1855
Porterfield female
Mary Patton, slave

P'S

Year of 1855
William P. B. Parkin
Francis Persinger
Ferdinand N. Piles
Eliza'th Parker
Milbon C. Peck

Year of 1856
Phillips son
Rebecca Susan Pine
Jane Pack
Eliza Angiline Perry

Year of 1857
Margaret A. H. Patton
Patton son
Jas. L. Prentice
Isaac Painter

Year of 1858
Allen, Peters slave
Elisha G. Peck
Margaret Peck
Loami Pack
Susan C. Peters
Malinda M. Peters

Year of 1859
Cynthia Peters

Year of 1860
Parker slave, Charles
Elizabeth Pugh
Jno A. Peters
Saml. E. Phillips
Buchanan Peck

Year of 1862
Elizabeth Phillips
Allen Pennington
Cynthia E. Peters
James, Pack slave
Elizabeth P. Pack
William B. Pack
Robert A. Pack
Esbers Ann Powell
Charles P. Parker
James Parker
Allen G. Piles
John B. Patton

Year of 1865
Harrison Pack
Andrew J. Peck
Elizabeth Pence

P'S

Year of 1866
Mary A. Parker

Year of 1867
Molly Patton
Sarah Parker
Alice Park
Virginia Pence

Year of 1868
John Peters

Year of 1869
Jacob Piles

Year of 1870
Samuel Pack
James I. Pack

R'S

Year of 1853
John William Reed
Eunice J. Ross
Mary E. Rutlege
Marion F. Ross
Haslet K. Riffe

Year of 1854
Henderson Rains
Eliza Rains
Leah Rains
Catharine Ryan
George Ryan

Year of 1855
Martha E. Rye
James H. Rye
Mary Rice
Andrew J. Roach
James A. Roach
Martha Ann Ripley

Year of 1856
Effie A. Rutledge
John Robertson
Rachael Riffe
Walter H. Riddle

Year of 1857
John Reaburn
Mary Reaburn
Luanaa--Riddle slave

R'S (continued)

Year of 1858
Thomas Floid Reynolds
Christopher C. Reynolds
Martha A. Rains
P. S. Rice

Year of 1859
Reaburn female
Amanda J. Ragland
Jackson Rains
Julia Rhine

Year of 1860
Adelia A. Reaburn
Mary A. Reynolds
Reed child
Mary S. Rice

Year of 1862
Marinda Riffe
Steven Ridgeway

Year of 1865
Geo Rollyson

Year of 1866
Ralston female
Emily J. Reed
Reed male
John Roles

Year of 1868
Ramsey mlae
Geo Rhyne
Benjamin Reed

Year of 1869
Mary E. Riffe
Arrena Rutlege

S'S

Year of 1856
Andrew Summers
Elizabeth Virginia Saunders
Samuel-Swope slave
Willis--Smith slave

Year of 1857
Mary Spade
John Scott
Elizabeth Steele
James Steele
Salina Saunders
Mary Syms

S'S (continued)

Year of 1857
Jacob Smith
Millard F. Smith
Robert Syms
Sarah A. Stevens

Year of 1858
Shirer male
Clarah Shiree
Clara A. Spangler
Nancy--Spangler slave
Aggy--Spangler slave
Jno. A. Spangler
Benjamin T. Spangler
Eliza A. Spangler
George A. Spangler
Mary E. Spangler
Rosa L. Spangler
George A. Spangler
John--Spangler slave
G. M. Spangler
Sarah E. Spangler
Rich'd D. Shanklin
William A. Shanklin
Elizabeth A. Shanklin
George Stevenson
Mary Stevenson

Year of 1859
Emily Smith
Margaret C. Sams
Sarah E. Scott
Enoch Shanklin

Year of 1860
Spangler slave--Albert
Seward L. Smith
Edith Steele
Martha Smith
Ugenia C. Smith
James W. Smith

Year of 1862
James A. Suttle
Valentine Shultz
Smith male
Eliza V. Spangler
Allen M. Smith
Amanda E. Skaggs
Lewis Saunders
Rebecca J. Saunders
Nancy A. Saunders
Sarah H. Saunders
Smith child
Eliza Shepherd
Sarah C. Shepherd

S'S (continued)

Year of 1862
Lillian Sonaker
Andrew E. Spangler
Newton K. Spangler
Amanda Shanklin
John W. Shirey

Year of 1865
Christopher Skaggs

Year of 1866
William H. Shanklin
Mary E. Scott
John Scott

Year of 1867
Shives child
Frances Smith

Year of 1868
Stover daughter
Shultz son
Shepherd son
Jane Spangler
Alonzo Smith

Year of 1869
Jane E. Smith
R. V. Shanklin
C. A. Spangler
James M. Spangler
Smith female
Geo. P. Suttle
Anna Smith
Margaret Smithson
Sarah Steele
William Henry Steele

Year of 1870
Rosa Smith

T'S

Year of 1853
Nancy Welch Terry
William Allen Thompson
Loami Thompson
Joseph Thrasher slave
Hetty Thrasher slave
James Thrasher slave
Brooker Thompson
William Taylor

T'S (continued)

Year of 1854
Emily Toler
Sarah J. Toler
Erastus Toler
William P. Tuggle
Margaret M. Tuggle
Elizabeth Thompson
John H. Trent
Elizabeth Tegairt

Year of 1855
Tabitha Terry

Year of 1856
Paulina Tomlinson
Sarah Comer Tuggle
Amanda R. Thomas

Year of 1857
David Tomlinson
Leonard Tunrer
Jno W. Taylor

Year of 1858
Elisabeth Tailor
James W. Townsly
Mary L. Tiffany
Sarah J. Tiffany
Andy J. Tiffany
Thomas F. Tiffany

Year of 1859
Francis C. Teays
Tiffany slave, Susan

Year of 1860
Alex'r P. Taylor
Erastus Terry

Year of 1862
Agnus T. Thomas
Jno A. Taylor
John W. Taylor

Year of 1865
William B. Thomas

Year of 1867
Taylor child
Geo. Thompson

Year of 1868
William W. tiffany
J. M. McD Tiffany
Thompson son

T'S (continued)

Year of 1868
Hannah Triplet

Year of 1869
Joseph McD Tiffany

Year of 1870
Isabel Tygrett

U'S

Year of 1853
Nancy Upton

Year of 1856
Joseph A. Upton

Year of 1860
Fleming Underwood
Edwary Underwood
Mary Underwood

V'S

Year of 1853
Lurenia Antionette Vance
Mary B. Vines
Bella Magdaline Vance

Year of 1854
Rebecca Jane Vass
Ebro Willy Vass

Year of 1855
George Vass
Minerva Vance

Year of 1860
Electra A. Vass
Vawter slave, Bartler
Margaret Vance

Year of 1862
George Viars
Isaac P. Vass
Mary J. Vawter

Year of 1868
Isabel C. Vanstavern

W'S

Year of 1853
Mary Jane Weaver
Harriet-Walker slave
Philip-Walker slave
Thomas Walker
Walker slave
Lucinda Wykle
Edwin W. Woodson
Sarah A. Walker

Year of 1854
Margaret Wikle
Martha A. Wiseman
Lewis Williams
Mary M. Wiseman
Thos J. Wiseman
Neivel J. Woodram
Georgiana Wayte
Mary E. Wiley

Year of 1855
George Watson
Adaliza Walker
Nathan H. Walker
Rachel B. Waring
Jacob Wickline
Caroly Wickline
John Woodram
Warner H. Webb

Year of 1856
Bird Clark Woodram
Felix Williams
Woodram male
Wiseman child

Year of 1857
Sarah Wickline
Cornelius--Woodville slave
Robert Willey

Year of 1858
Warlopa--Indian
Felix Williams
Felming W. Warren
Marlin V. Wheeler
Sarah Woodram

Year of 1859
Winebinner female
Waite female
Mary M. Wickline
Sarah Jane Wylie
Thornton F. Warren
Jas M. Williams

W'S (Continued)

Year of 1860
Jacob Wickline
Mary Wickline
Woodville slave--Peter
Rebecca Workman
Anna Wicle
John W. Wicle
Emily E. Wiseman
Jos V. Walker
John A. Wood

Year of 1862
Zac F. Wikle
Fiel--Walker slave
Permelia Workman
Dickson Walker
William M. Wickline
Andrew J. Weiss
Robert Wickline
Charles L. Wiseman
Sarah V. Waite

Year of 1865
James F. Watts
Arabel Jane Wickle
Leroy Wood
Virginia E. Wilson
Joseph Wilson
Samuel Wood

Year of 1866
David J. Wickline
Margaret White

Year of 1867
Walker child
Andrew Walker

Year of 1868
Emmeline Wikle

Year of 1869
Simon P. Wills
Isa Walter

Year of 1870
Helene Wylie
James Wickline

Y'S

Year of 1853
Nicholas Young
Sarah Ann Young

Year of 1854
James Young

Year of 1855
Yates male

Year of 1858
Susannah Young

Year of 1859
Margaret L. Young
Ann Eliza Young

Year of 1860
Susan Young

Year of 1862
William G. Young
Oseola Young

Year of 1866
Jane Young
Young male

Year of 1870
Robert Young

END OF

INDEX

www.ingramcontent.com/pod-product-compliance
Lightning Source LLC
Chambersburg PA
CBHW080335270326
41927CB00014B/3231